THE

# FREEMASONS.

## WHAT THEY ARE—WHAT THEY DO—WHAT THEY ARE AIMING AT.

FROM THE FRENCH OF MGR. SEGUR,

Author of "Plain Talk," etc.

BOSTON:

**PUBLISHED BY PATRICK DONAHOE.**

1869.

IMPRIMATUR.

JOANNES JOSEPHUS,

EPISCOPUS BOSTON.

# PREFACE.

This short treatise written, not by the Archbishop of Paris, as carelessly stated by some newspapers, but by Mgr. de Ségur, the author of the work lately translated and published under the title of " Plain Talk," was composed to unveil and show Freemasonry, *as it is in the Old World.* Its strictures, therefore, are not wholly applicable to Freemasonry, as it is in the United States. Yet, Masons here may read it with profit to themselves ; and those who are not Masons, but might be tempted to join some Lodge, will, it is hoped, abandon the idea, if they read this book. Even here, Freemasonry is a Secret Society ; and to become a member of it, one must take at least an oath, and swear by the name of God, to do so-and-so. Now, God's command is : " Thou shalt not take the name of the Lord thy God in vain." And surely, it is taken in vain by American Freemasons, because they take it without any sufficient and justifiable cause. For, apart from other ends of their Society, and especially that of affording members a chance never to want what assistance they may need in case of a momentary difficulty in their affairs, or loss of means, or health,— the main object seems to be to meet at times, in order to spend an afternoon in a merry way, and to partake of banquets, provided for the occasion. But where is the necessity to bind oneself by an oath, to gather now and then round a bountifully supplied table, or even to be charitable ; and, for such purposes, to be a member of a *Secret* Society ? We have many benevolent societies ; there is no secret about them, no oath to be taken by those who wish to be members of them. Their object is to carry out the principles of Christian Charity ; to that they bind themselves simply by a promise, as also to contribute so much for the purposes of the Society.

There are other objections to joining Freemasonry, even here ; but this is not the place to discuss that subject.

The French work, here offered in an English garb, contains expressions which it is impossible to translate.

In the very first page, we have the French word *Franc*, which means *frank* and *freed*, not *free*. The literal translation, if the meaning of the word is to be given, of *Franc-Maçon*, should be *Freed*, not *Free-mason* ;— freed from the taxes and imposts to be paid to any government what-

ever, the first *Franc-Maçons* having been so called, because owing to the help they gratuitously
gave towards building our grand old Catholic
Cathedrals, their corporations were exempted,
*freed* for a time from paying the taxes due to
Government.

The French word *les profanes* had to be translated by the English word *profane men*, or simply
*the profane*. Yet, *profane*, in English, is generally applied to a man who uses profane language ;
in French, it means, as used in this work, a man
not worthy, or, at least, not yet fit — to be a
member of a Society — an outsider.

The French word *Arrière Loges*, has been ren-
dered by " Back Lodges." Now, this does not
seem to convey the meaning of the French ex-
pression, which carries an allusion to the back
part of a shop, or of a theatre, where matters
are so different from what they appear in the
Store or on the Scene.

The reader will often meet with the word *Obedience*. The French word *Obédience* means here
a certain portion of territory, a district, a number of individuals and corporations put under
the jurisdiction of a Superior who commands,
and to whom consequently *obedience* is due.
Hence, the whole has been summed up, in French,
in the word *Obédience*.

Again, in the 28th chapter, the *Mason-sister* is spoken of as *tournant à la Sœur grise*, literally, *turning by degrees Grey Sister*. But the adjective *gris*, the feminine of which is *grise*, means *grey*, and also *slightly intoxicated :* and the witty point of it is, that a Grey Sister is a venerable person, member of the Community of Grey Nuns, whereas a woman, even slightly intoxicated, is surely anything but a respectable person; and the idea of a *Mason-sister* turning *Grey Nun*, brings a smile to the lips, the more so, that the idea is presented by a word, the *true* meaning of which in the case cannot be mistaken.

Some comparisons have been retained and literally translated; in their English dress, they may look somewhat queer and awkward ; yet, it is supposed by the translator, that any intelligent reader will understand them at once.

SOUTH BOSTON, *Oct. 2d*, 1868.
*Feast of the Guardian Angels.*

# TABLE OF CONTENTS.

# CONTENTS.

# THE FREEMASONS.

In this short treatise, I do not examine Free-masonry in its political, nor even in its social bearings ; my sole object is to lead to the understanding of its dangers in the moral and religious point of view.

A fearful propagandism, which is increasing from day to day, and covers as with an immense network not Europe alone, but the whole world, renders watchfulness and resistance more and more necessary. There is hardly any Diocese in which Freemasons are not organized. From their own last accounts, they number *eight millions,* and have about *five thousand* lodges, not counting the back

or occult ones.   In France, the number of
Freemasons already exceeds *one million six
hundred thousand.*

To make Freemasonry known, is the best
means to hold away from it well-disposed persons.   I then offer this short treatise for the
people, to Clergymen, and to the zealous Catholics who take to heart the holy cause of the
Church, and the preservation of Faith.   May
it help them to keep from the fire many imprudent butterflies who rush to the candle,
because they do not know that it burns !


## I.

### The Name Freemason.

Generally, names indicate the nature of
things.   Here, it is quite the reverse: Freemasons are neither free, nor Masons.   That
they are not Masons. needs no proof.   That
they are not free (*franc*) is no less clear; for
their society rests on secrets, on mysterious
initiations, which they must not reveal to
any one, under penalty of death.

To outsiders, Freemasons make it appear

that they are simply a merry and philanthropic, eating, drinking, singing and beneficent society. We are going to see if there is not something else under that. They are not any more harmless than they are Masons.

If *"Francmaçon,"* means *Freemason*, the veil drawn over the association is to some extent lifted up: *free*, but what is their freedom? *free* towards whom? *free* to do what? We shall soon see it: and these are fearful mysteries.

This queer name of Freemason comes to them, it seems, from Scotland. After the most just suppression, by Pope Clement V., and the King of France, Philippe-le-Bel, at the beginning of the 14th Century, of the Order of Templars,[1] some of these infamous men

[1] The Knights-Templars had been instituted to defend the Faith in the Holy Land. They soon spread all over Europe; and, by their wealth, acquired an immense influence. One of their Grand-Masters allowed himself to be seduced by the Turks, and introduced into the Order, with habits against nature, sacrilegious practices which too long remained a deep secret. Philippe-le-Bel discovered those horrible mysteries, and strongly urged Pope Clement V. to punish the Templars, and to suppress their Order. The main object

fled to Scotland, where they constituted
themselves a secret society, vowing implacable hatred and undying vengeance against
Popes and Kings. The better to disguise
their plottings, they affiliated themselves to
a corporation of masons, adopted their insignia and slang, and later, spread all over Europe, with the help of Protestantism. Their
final organization dates, it seems, from the
first years of the eighteenth century.

To throw dust in the eyes of the people,
they pretended to date back as far as the
Temple of Solomon,— the Tower of Babel,—
the Flood, — aye, even the Terrestrial Paradise ; and many of their adepts were simple
enough to believe those silly stories.

What then is Freemasonry ? How does
one become a Freemason ? What takes
place in the Lodges ? Behind the Lodges are

---

of Philippe-le-Bel, was to confiscate their goods and
chattels for his own benefit, whereas the Pope's object
was the interest of Faith, justice and morality. Many
Templars were acquitted ; others, severely punished ;
some of them, the most guilty, were given up to the
secular power; others escaped and fled. This historical point has at present become an ascertained and
clear fact.

there back Lodges, and what is carried on
in them? Is Freemasonry a praiseworthy,
religious, or at least, beneficent institution?
Is it not essentially anti-christian, anti-cath-
olic? Is it powerful and active? What
does it aim at? Is it lawful to enroll oneself under its mysterious flag? We intend
answering briefly these grave questions.[1]
But before proceeding, let us lay down an
important distinction.

## II.

### THERE IS FREEMASON AND FREEMASON.

There is the Freemasonry which is seen
more or less, and the Freemasonry which is
not seen at all; and the two make but one:
" Freemasonry is one, its starting point is
one," said lately a certain *Brother* Ragon,
one of the standard organs of the sect.[2]

---

[1] A large part of our information has been taken
from the interesting work of Mr. Alex. de St. Albin,
entitled: " *The Freemasons and the Secret Societies.*"
It should be consulted by readers anxious to go deeper
into the study of this important question.

[2] He has written a book, which has been by order

To the former belongs the immense majority of the Freemasons. Out of the eight
millions of adepts " there are hardly five
hundred thousand active members." This
explicit acknowledgment the *Masonic World*
newspaper let out in its number for August,
1866.

Those five hundred thousand are the Masons on the active service list, the picked
Masons; still they are not yet the Masons of
the back Lodges,—the impious Masons, who
know what they are doing; who deliberately
work to destroy Christianity, Church and Society; and who, under different names, constitute what is called Secret Societies. They
are the head of the Revolution which purposes, as known by all, to overturn the world,
and to substitute everywhere "the rights of

of the Chapter Lodge, Orient of Nancy, the object of
" an official reprint called *Sacred Edition*," for the exclusive use of the Lodges and Masons. This Br∴.
Ragon is an Ex-Venerable. The Grand-Orient, in his
approbation of his writings, has proclaimed that they
contain the pure Masonic Doctrine. We shall often,
in this treatise, quote his words, as an authentic source
not to be disowned by our adversaries.

man to the rights and to the kingdóm of God."

The eight millions of members of *exterior* Freemasonry are nearly to a man blindfolded individuals, who, most of the time, know not whither they are led. They are used as a reserve corps from which recruits are selected, — as good milch cows which can be milked at will, — as trumpeters who sing everywhere the praises of Freemasonry, who extend its influence, and draw to it sympathy . . . . and money.

Behind that multitude who drink, sing, and talk morality, the real Masons marvellously hide all their plots.

Among the members of *exterior* Freemasonry, there may be, and doubtless there are, persons of worldly honorableness, warmhearted and generous, who would be Christians, did they know religion, but ignorance leads them astray. They are caught by appearances of brotherhood and beneficence, and in good faith feel indignant when the Church denounces and condemns the Masonic Order.

But the largest number of Freemasons is

made up of the rich and poor among the *common people*,—deluded persons, led by the nose, and readily hunted upon scent by leaders of sects; they are utterly amazed when they come to discover the depth of the pit, which they have dug with their own hands.

There are also among Freemasons, numerous ambitious men, lawyers without suits-at-law and conscience, unsound minds, revolutionary people, ideologists in search of *The Unknown*, philanthropists after the fashion of the day; finally, and mostly, men of pleasure, who are very willing to be made to speak a would-be morality, and to save mankind, by eating, drinking, and singing. Freemasonry counts very many army men; also Jews and tavern-keepers. In Paris, alone, nearly two thousand tavern-keepers *piously* attend the Lodges.

Whilst granting that here and there good men have strayed into the ranks of Freemasonry, still, we shall be forced to say, after having dived into its mysteries, that if there are any, they are very few.

## III.

### WHAT IS THE SECRET OF THE CUSTOMARY RECRUITING OF FREEMASONRY?

It may be truly said that it is the secret of the Devil.  Listen, and judge.

" The main point," wrote one of the occult Chiefs, surnamed " Little Tiger," " is to iso-late man from his family, and to make him give up family habits.  Man is well inclined, by a natural tendency, to shrink from the cares of the household, to go after easy pleas-ures, and forbidden enjoyments.  He likes the long chatting of the Coffee-house, and the idleness of the Theatre.  Draw him, drag him away ; let him fancy himself of some impor-tance ; teach him discreetly to loathe his daily avocation ; and, through that game, after hav-ing separated him from wife and children after having shown him how heavy are all du-ties, put into his head to wish for another mode of life.  Man was born a rebel ; fan that spirit of rebellion to the burning point, but let it not blaze into a fire. This is the preparation for the great work which you must now begin.

When you will have instilled into some souls a dislike of family and Religion (one almost always follows the other), drop some words to bring about a wish to be affiliated to the nearest Lodge. The feeling of vanity, urging common people to identify themselves with Freemasonry, is something so silly, and yet so universal, that I am always wondering at man's stupidity. I am surprised not to see all men knocking at the doors of the Venerables, and asking from those gentlemen the honor to be one of the workmen chosen for the rebuilding of Solomon's Temple. The prestige of the Unknown has on men such a power, that they prepare themselves with fear for the fantastical trials of initiation, and of the brotherly banquet.

To be members of a Lodge, to feel one's self called to keep — wife and children being excluded — a secret which is never trusted to you, is for certain natures, a delight and an object of ambition." [1]

[1] Letter to the Lodge of Piedmont, Jan., 18th, 1822,

What do you say to this, reader? What wickedness!

Another Mason, Br ∴[1] Clavel, sets forth, although in a less cynical way, the same honest system of recruiting. Here are his own words. God must be blessed that those impious men at times betray the secret of their conspiracy: "Freemasonry, *we say to those whom we want to enroll*, is a progressive, philanthropic institution, the members of which live like brothers, under the level of a pleasing equality.

" A Freemason is a citizen of the universe; there is not a place where he will not meet brothers eager to welcome him, without need of any other recommendation but his title, without making himself known except by the signs and the mysterious words adopted by the initiated.

" To bring to a decisive step those led by curiosity, *we add* that our Society religiously

[1] These three dots form the mysterious triangle symbol of the equalizing *level* which Freemasonry means to carry round about all parts of the world, to eradicate from them all religion and all authority not emanating from the Masonic Order.

keeps a secret which belongs, and can belong, only to Freemasons.

" To the same end, *we give* to men of pleasure *glowing accounts* of the frequent banquets in which rich diet and generous wines excite mirth, and tie tighter the bonds of brotherly intimacy.

"As to working men and merchants, *we tell them* that Freemasonry will be very profitable to them, by enlarging the sphere of their transactions, and increasing the number of their customers. Thus *have we arguments for all inclinations, for all vocations, for all minds, for all classes.*" [1]

Once more, honest reader, what do you say to that ?

To give a last touch to the picture, we might add : As to practical Christians, not to frighten them away, the Masons amuse them with fine words; *they tell them* that Freemasonry excludes no Religion ; that even Priests are members of it, etc.

Did not a good old lady, a mother of a family, come once to consult a holy Priest, a

[1] Picturesque History of Freemasonry. pp. 1-2.

friend of mine, and to ask him most seriously, was it true " that the Dominican Fathers were at the head of Freemasonry in France ? They plague my husband to seek for admission," she added, "and as I oppose it with all my might, some came to tell me that the Dominican Fathers belonged to that Society, and governed it. Is it really so ? "

Such are the honest secrets of the recruiting in the Freemasonry.

## IV.

### WITH WHAT CEREMONIES ONE IS MADE A FREE-MASON.

When one of those " certain natures " has been entrapped by any of the managers, here is the result. It is as grotesque as it is culpable ; and this is not saying little.

The first degree of " exterior " Freemasonry is the degree of *Apprentice;* the second, that of *Companion;* the third, that of *Master-Mason.* *Degree* here means *degree* of ascension towards light; of course we Christians, men of faith and common sense, we are simply *profane*—doomed to darkness.

The first step, then, is to apply to become an *Apprentice-mason.* On the day appointed for admission, the candidate, " brought to the Lodge by a *Brother* unknown to him," is shown to a solitary room, where he finds, between two lights, the Bible opened at the first Chapter of St. John. Why so? An uninitiated Mason would answer: " Because we are a religious and enlightened people ; " but what answer would an initiated Mason give, — a Mason of those back Lodges, of which mention is to be made hereafter, in which they bluntly tell you that there is no other God but Nature, and that Freemasonry worships the Sun ?

The candidate is left alone for a few minutes; waiting enhances the interest of the proceedings. His clothes are taken from him ; the left side and the right knee are exposed naked ; he slips one shoe on (this is of the utmost importance) ; they take from him his hat, and sword (he must have one), and " metal," that is, his money. He is hoodwinked, and led to the " closet of reflection ;" he is forbidden to remove his hoodwink before he hears three loud raps. Again he is left alone ; and some time is spent in

that kind of uneasy waiting caused in the
simpleton by that series of mysterious do-
ings.   At last he hears the signal; quickly he
removes his hoodwink, and finds himself in a
hall hung in black; and on the walls he reads,
with what satisfaction one can readily understand, encouraging inscriptions like the following:

*" If you are addicted to dissembling, trem-
ble !  We shall read the very bottom of your
heart.  If fear has smitten your soul, dare not
go any farther.  The heaviest sacrifices, even
that of life, may be expected of you ; are you
ready for them? "* etc.

In this " closet of reflection," the candidate is obliged to make his last will, and
to answer *in writing* the following questions :

" What are the duties of Man towards
God?" " What are his duties towards his fel-
low-men ? " " What are his duties towards
himself? "

Then Br. ·. *Terrible* (*sic*) takes with the
point of a sword the last will and the three
answers, to carry them to the Lodge.   In the
Freemason cant, *Lodge* means the meeting
of the adepts; the place for meeting is call-

ed *Temple* (*pious* remembrance of the Templars and their mysteries); the President is called *Venerable*.

Br.·. *Terrible* brings to the Venerable the last will and the answers. No matter what the answers are, the candidate is always accepted. The atheist, blasphemer Proudhon, was admitted when he had just answered, "Justice to all men," — "devotedness to one's country," — "*war against God!*" True, it was the Lodge of "sincerity, perfect union, and lasting friendship." So sweet a Lodge could not refuse a candidate so perfectly sincere, so sincerely perfect.

Br.·. *Terrible* then comes back to the poor candidate, hoodwinks him again, and puts around his neck a rope, the end of which he holds, thus to lead him to the door of the *Temple* against which he makes him give three hard raps. Those inside try not to laugh.

The *Temple* is hung in blue, — what passes there being all heavenly. A Br.·. called *First Inspector* gravely announces to the Venerable, that there are raps at the door. Here ensues a dialogue between the Venerable, the First Inspector and Br .·. *Terrible;* after which the candidate is introduced into the Temple. There are two columns, between which he is brought, the rope round his neck all the while. Br .·. *Terrible* fraternally presses the point of his sword against the candidate's breast, and then begin the questions.

The Venerable, putting his spectacles on his venerable nose, says, in a gloomy, but venerable voice: "What do you feel? What do you see?" Rather indelicate questions to put to a poor devil who is hoodwinked, and whose flesh is pricked by a sword.

The postulant candidly: "I see nothing, but I feel the point of a sword."

The Venerable: "Reflect deeply on the step you are taking; you are going to undergo terrible trials. Do you feel fortitude enough to brave all the dangers to which you may be exposed?"

The postulant, with energy: "Yes, sir!"

The Venerable, without laughing: "Well, then, I give you up! Br .·. *Terrible,* drag this profane out of the *Temple,* and take him to all places through which must pass the mor-

2

tal who seeks the honor to know our secrets."
All this is textual, as is also whatever we
shall say next.    It is copied from the Masonic Ritual, lately reprinted with great care.

Forthwith Br . ⁚. *Terrible* draws the rope,
drags the candidate, who is all this time
hoodwinked, makes him whirl about half a
dozen times in a hall called " the pacing Hall."
When he supposes him bewildered, he slyly
brings him back to the Lodge, the candidate
not being aware of it.

Look out ! the  trials are about to begin.
It would be Jocrisse's martyrdom, were it
not the initiation to abominable things.


## V.


### FIRST AND TERRIBLE TRIAL OF THE APPREN-
### TICE-MASON.


In the centre of the Lodge is prepared
a big frame, covered with paper, as those
hoops through which pass horsewomen in
a circus.  *Brothers* hold up that frame, the
instrument of the first trial

"What is to be done with this profane?" asks Br.·. *Terrible* of the Venerable. The Venerable replies: "Lead him into the cave." Immediately two Masons seize upon the postulant, throw him with all their strength on the frame, the paper of which tearing lets him pass. Two other Masons receive him on their arms. The two folds of the door are banged with great force; and, from the imitation of the noise of bolts and locks, the intelligent candidate may fancy himself shut in the famous cave. . . . some moments are spent in a deep silence, the silence of the grave!

Suddenly the Venerable (sneezes,) gives a loud rap with his mallet (on no matter what), directs the aspirant to kneel, and offers a kind of prayer to the Patron of the Institution, whom they call "the grand Architect of the Universe." Freemasonry is profusely lavish of that sort of prayer; it puts God's holy name everywhere. Infamous hypocrisy! for, we shall see, presently, that, in reality, Freemasonry is Atheist, and that "*the worship of Nature is the Mason's purpose,*" as the sacred author dares to publish it in one of his official books. [1]

The Venerable orders the aspirant, still hoodwinked, to sit on a chair strewn with points (for greater comfort), and asks him does he persevere in his *noble* purpose? The simpleton majestically answers, Yes. Then follow silly questions on morals, and a pathetic discourse by the Venerable on the duties of Masons, the first of which, he says, "is to preserve an absolute silence on the secrets of Freemasonry." We shall soon see if those secrets are in harmony with all their ludicrous ceremonies: and, moreover, why any secret in a society which calls itself purely beneficent and philanthropic?

Now begins another comedy; the Venerable asks the aspirant if he is sincere, and if he can affirm it on his word of honor? He orders "the Br.·. Sacrificer" to lead the candidate to "the altar," and to make him drink from a cup which a pivot separates into two compartments. "If you are not sincere," says the Venerable, "the sweetness of

[1] Br.·. Ragon : Philosophical and Interpretative Treatise on Ancient and Modern Initiations.

this beverage will soon be changed for you into subtle poison." And by means of the pivot, he is made to drink, without perceiving the trick, first pure water, and next a bitter draught. Of course he is still hoodwinked, and still makes wry faces. At once, the Venerable, who is smarter than he looks, exclaims, striking again with his gavel: " What do I see, sir? What signifies this sudden change in your features? Is it that the sweet beverage has already turned for you into poison? . . . let the profane be removed !"

Br.·. *Terrible* brings back the postulant between the two columns. The Venerable has a last word for him: " If you intend deceiving us, hope not to succeed in it; better for you to withdraw at once; you are still free. Were we to become convinced of your perfidy, it would be fatal to you; and you should have *to lose the hope of ever seeing again the light of the day.* Br.·. *Terrible,* put back this profane on the chair of reflection."

Should the postulant decide to proceed, he is subjected to a second trial.

## VI.

### The Three Journeys. A Second Trial of the Apprentice-Mason.

At the sight of millions of men submitting for centuries to these humiliating and ridiculous practices, one is seized with compassion; and, like Br .·. *Little Tiger*, "one is amazed at the stupidity of mankind." Were it not that the Devil interferes, not a man of sense could submit to so childish and nonsensical phantasmagories. No one could believe that men endowed with reason, and who all boast more or less of being freethinkers, practise those absurd rites, if it were not an absolutely certain fact, and were not the Ritual, printed by the sect, before us, to render doubt impossible.

The first "journey" consists in going three times round the Lodge, prepared for that express purpose. The candidate, still hoodwinked, and led by Br .·. *Terrible*, walks in succession on movable floors, which being

set on rollers, and full of rough spots, pass
from under his feet; next on swinging floors,
which suddenly give way under him, and
seem to let him fall in an abyss. Then he is
made to go up "the endless ladder;" if he
wishes to stop, he is told to ascend still; until having ascended (at least he thinks so) to
a very great height, he is commanded to
throw himself down . . . and he falls from an
elevation of three feet!!! During all that
time, the initiators simulate the sounds of
high winds, hail and thunder, cries of infants,
and a dreadful din generally. Thus ends the
first "journey." Truly, it is too stupid!

The second "journey" resembles the first,
and the third resembles the second: a repetition of the same gross buffooneries, of the
same heroism on the part of the candidate.
Between each journey the Venerable makes
pretence of doubting the aspirant's courage;
he exhorts him not to continue, and the other
still continues.

There is, however, some novelty introduced
in the third "journey;" as it was done to
Don Quixote and to Sancho, likewise hoodwinked, and on the famous wooden horse,

so pretended purificatory flames are passed under the nose of the unfortunate aspirant. "Let him pass through the purifying flames," has thundered the Venerable, "in order that nothing profane remain in him!" And, in fact, whilst the postulant gravely descends the steps of the Orient (it is the place where sits the Venerable) to go between the two columns, Br .·. *Terrible* envelopes him thrice in flames produced by means of I don't know what gas and what powder prepared for the occasion.

To think that men at all ages, of all conditions, that men of learning, members of academies, officers, generals, Marshals of France, men in high places, fathers of family, men belonging to the best society have passed, now pass, and will still pass through all that! It bewilders one; and it is humiliating for mankind.

But we are not done yet; and the postulant is not yet a Mason.

## VII.

### THE FINAL TRIALS.

"Profane man," says the Venerable, "you have been purified by the earth, the air, the water, and the fire. I cannot praise your courage too highly; yet let it not forsake you; you have still other trials to undergo. *The Society into which you desire to be admitted, will, perhaps, demand that you should shed for it even the last drop of your blood. Are you ready?*" Thus, for the second time he is warned that to be a Freemason, one must bind oneself solemnly to *all* that the interests of Freemasonry may require: one must be ready to sacrifice one's life, at the first word.

On the affirmative answer of the postulant, the Venerable adds: "We must convince you that this is not a mere matter of form. Are you willing to have a vein opened this minute?" The postulant consents, and forthwith a slight scratch is made on his arm.

There is a noise of trickling blood simulateα, and the arm is put in a sling.

The Venerable then proposes to him to impress upon his breast *the Masonic Seal*, by means of a hot iron. The aspirant again consents, and they apply to his breast either the hot side of a candle just put out, or a small glass slightly warmed with burning paper. At last, the aspirant must tell in a low tone of voice to " Br. ∴. Hospitaller" the amount of the offering he intends to make for indigent Masons.

Thus end the famous trials.

The Venerable lectures the aspirant with a terrible speech, and praises him for his courage in that emphatical and hollow style, the practice of which is religiously preserved by Freemasonry; and, as a reward for his heroism, he orders the Br. ∴. Master of Ceremonies " to initiate him to the degree of Apprentice, by teaching him . . . . to take the first step in the angle of an oblong square ! ! ! You will make him take the two other steps," adds he gravely, " and you will lead him afterwards to the altar of oaths." The three steps in the angle of an oblong square constitute, in fact, the *walk of an Apprentice Mason*. The man who has allowed himself to be hoodwinked, pricked in the breast, thrown through the papered frame in the cave, who has swallowed clear water, slided, jumped, etc., in his three journeys, who has ascended *the endless ladder*, and has heroically dared to fall from the height of three feet; who was purified by the exploding powder, has shed his noble blood, has promised and heard so many fine things, that man is at last initiated to something serious: he has been taught " to walk three steps in the angle of an oblong square ! "

## VIII.

### THE OATH.

Before the oath is taken, there is another short ceremony. The neophyte, still hood-winked, is " led to the altar of oaths," where he kneels down, whilst the Br .·. Master of Ceremonies puts on his left breast the point of a compass. On the altar is a Bible opened, and on the Bible a flaming sword.

" Up, and to order, Brethren," exclaims the Venerable; " the neophyte is going to take the awful oath." Awful, truly; this time, joking ceases, and we have true Freemasonry. All the assistants arise, draw their swords, and the postulant takes the impious oath as follows:

" I swear, in the name of the Supreme Architect of all the worlds, never to reveal the secrets, the signs, the grasps, the words, the doctrines and the customs of the Freemasons, and to preserve thereon an eternal silence. I promise and swear to God never to betray any part of them, neither by writings, signs, words, nor gestures; never to cause any of them to be written, lithographed or printed; never to publish anything of what has been confided to me up to this time, or is to be in future. I pledge and submit myself to the following penalty, if I break my word: That my lips be burnt with a hot iron; that my hands be cut off; that my tongue be plucked out; that my throat be cut; that my corpse be hung in a Lodge during the work of admission of a new brother, as a branding of my unfaithfulness, and a warning to others; that it be then burnt, and the ashes scattered to the winds, so that there may remain no trace of the memory of my treason.   So help me God, and this holy Gospel. Amen."

Those unfortunate men thus use the name of God and of the Gospel in their detestable oaths, and give themselves up, hands and feet bound, to a hidden power, which they know not, nor shall ever know; which shall command them to kill, and they must kill; to violate divine and human laws, and if they do not obey, they must die! Can an upright man, I do not say a Christian, but simply an upright man, in the least strict sense of the word, can he, I ask, take the oath of a Freemason?

After the oath, the postulant is led back between the two columns. All the Brothers (what Brothers!) surround him, forming a circle, and turn towards him their drawn swords, "so that he be like a centre from which rays are darting." The Master of Ceremonies, standing behind, is ready to take the hoodwink from his eyes, whilst another Brother, standing in front, brings under the nose of the unhappy neophyte, the lamp and the inflammable powder, used before for the purifying flames.

The comedy is again performed.

"Do you judge this aspirant worthy to be admitted among us?" asks the Venerable to the Br.·. *First Overseer*. "Yes, Venerable," answers he. "What do you ask for him?"

" Light." And the Venerable, in a solemn tone of voice: " Let there be light !" He gives three heavy raps with the mallet. At the third rap, the bandage falls, the powder explodes, and the neophyte, all dazzled, . . . . surely sees nothing but fire. Then he notices, to his great delight, all the drawn swords pointing to his breast, and all his excellent Brothers exclaim altogether: " May God punish the traitor !" " Fear nothing, Brother," says the Venerable, " fear nothing from these swords pointed towards you. They are threatening traitors only. If you are faithful to Freemasonry, as we have the right to hope, these swords shall ever be ready to protect you. If, on the contrary, you ever betrayed it, *no spot on earth could offer you a shelter against these avenging weapons.*"

By his order, the new Brother is brought back to the Altar; again he is made to kneel (before whom ? before what ?), and the Venerable, taking on the altar (the altar of whom ?) the glistening sword, puts its point on the new Brother's head, and consecrates him " Apprentice-Mason," telling him : " In the name of the Great Architect of the Universe, and by virtue of the powers entrusted to me, I create and constitute you Apprentice-Mason and member of this respectable Lodge." Then, setting him up, he girds him with a white skin apron, gives him a pair of white gloves, which the Mason must wear in the Lodge as an emblem of his innocence!!! and, whether he be married or not, a pair of woman's gloves, which he must "offer to the one whom *he will esteem* the most." We soon shall see that there are *female Freemasons*, and that the worship of women is far from being proscribed from among those pure children of the "Great Architect of all the worlds." Finally, the Venerable reveals to the Apprentice, the signs, pass-words, and secrets peculiar to his degree, and gives him the treble brotherly kiss.— I do not know what are those special secrets ; for, according to the Ritual of the Mother Lodge of the Three Globes (sic), it is expressly said that "hints only, but never a full explanation, are given to the Apprentice; because *the smallest part* could not be fully explained and understood, unless the whole be presented and mastered."

Be this as it may, the initiation is proclaimed; the whole Lodge applauds; and the new Mason, having donned again his dress, is installed in his place. " Br∴ *Orator*" delivers to him a speech which ends this sacrilegious phantasmagoria.

## IX.

### OF THE DEGREE OF COMPANION, THE SECOND MASONIC DEGREE.

The second degree of *exterior* Freemasonry, is the degree of *Companion-mason*. When a poor Apprentice is tired of learning nothing new, he hopes to be initiated to something by becoming a Companion. Here are the proceedings:

The postulant Apprentice is no more hoodwinked; for, he has asked for light, and powder has been thrown in his eyes. He comes to knock as an Apprentice at the door of the Lodge.[1] The Venerable admits him,

[1] That is (at least in the Scotch Rite), two raps are given rapidly and tolerably loud, and, after a short

questions him, and orders him to go five times round the Lodge, accompanied by the Br∴. *Master of Ceremonies.* These are called "the mysterious journeys."

Then he makes him strike three times with a mallet on a rough stone (let him who can, understand). This is called the last work of an Apprentice. The Venerable pretends to explain to him the meaning of a glittering star, painted on a piece of canvas stretched on the floor; he tells him that it is "the symbol of that sacred fire, of that portion of divine light out of which the Grand Architect of the Universe has formed our souls," (which is a right down heresy, and strongly smells of Pantheism). Whether he understood or not, the Apprentice is led to the altar, as on the first occasion, and there, on his knees, he takes again the oath of Masonic fidelity, that horrible oath, condemned by all laws, divine and human.

halt, a third one, more gently. The *Companion* gives, in the same way, first two raps, then one, then two again. The *Master* gives three times the raps given by the Apprentice. The *Venerable*, or Master of the Lodge, gives, in an Olympian way, one loud rap only. It is Jupiter who strikes.

3

He is then proclaimed *Companion*,— the
Lodge applauding,— and led, not this time
" towards the East," as when received an
Apprentice, but " to the head of the column
of the South," where he has to listen to another speech from " Br .·. *Orator*." All this
is so silly, that one is tempted to grow angry,
rather than to laugh. And there are in
France, sixteen hundred thousand persons,
the most of them learned and literary men,
who have passed under that " Caudium yoke "
of the Secret Societies ! And in the whole
world, there are eight millions of them !

## X.

### Of the Third Degree, the Degree of Master-Mason.

We are all the while writing exclusively
about exterior Freemasonry ; the degree of
Master-mason is the third and last, the dignity
of Grand-Orient, and the other accessory
dignities which compose the exterior council
of the Masonic Order, not being degrees
properly speaking. A General, who has been

appointed Secretary of War, has not, for that, risen to a higher degree; he is invested with a dignity and a greater authority, but it ends there. Thus the Mason, when appointed Grand-Orient, is a Master-mason like all others, although he has been invested with the exterior command of all the Lodges of one obedience.

There are, in fact, in Freemasonry, various rites or obediences, which differ but very little one from the other. In France, we possess three Masonic rites: *The rite of the Grand-Orient of France; the Scotch rite,* of which the Grand-master is an old Academician; and a third rite, called *the Misraim rite.* Misraim is the name which cabalistic science has always given to a very powerful and very wicked demon. The Misraim rite acknowledges as its father the *pious* Cham, the accursed son of Noah.

But let us come back to our Companion who is so anxious to pass Master. The ceremonial becomes more and more solemn. The Lodge itself is not called any more a Lodge, but *the Room of the Centre.* The Celestial Chinese empire, is also called *the Empire of*

*the Centre.* This *Room of the Centre* then is
hung in black (in token of light and joy ?),
with skulls, whole skeletons, and bones embroidered in white, no doubt by the female
Freemasons " who are the most esteemed "
by the Masons of that *Centre.*

A candle of yellow wax (note it well: yellow) put in the East (not in the West, or else
all would be spoiled), and a dark lantern,
made of a skull, which lets light pass only
through the sockets, are placed on the altar
of the Venerable. The Venerable is Venerable no more. In this very respectable *Centre,* he is henceforth called the " Most Worshipful of the Room of the Centre." This
" Room of the Centre " and its Most Worshipful receive light in proportion with their
needs from the yellow candle and the skull-
lantern. In the middle of " the Room of the
Centre," whoever has a good eyesight, makes
out (oh, for the pure joys of Freemasonry !)
a coffin ! Yes a coffin, a true coffin; and this
coffin contains either a Mason or a manikin
(no matter which); according to Br . ∴ . *Clavel*
" it must be the last received Master." The
Ritual does not say, if, in his coffin, this last

received Master relishes the joke. I suppose he would rather be "the Most Worshipful."

To console him, they put a square on his head, an open compass on his feet, and over him, a branch of acacia (no doubt to keep off dew). All the Br.·. *Masters* are dressed, not in yellow, but in black; in the cheerfullest of the Lodges, they wear a black apron with a skull skilfully embroidered on the thighs. Finally, to complete their dress, they all wear hanging from the left shoulder to the right side, a wide blue ribbon, on which are embroidered, the sun, the moon and the stars. And do you know why they are thus decked up in their "Room of the Centre?" Listen to the Most Worshipful: "For what purpose do we meet?" he asks. "To find again the Master's word which is lost," gravely answers Br.·. *First Overseer.* The Most Worshipful then commands a search for "the word." Yet, every one seems to know it; for it is asked of all, and from all it is brought back to him. "How old are you?" inquires the Most Worshipful from Br.·. *First Overseer.* "Seven years, innocently answers he, no one knows why. A Master-Mason is always

" seven years old ; " it is the age of candor !
" What time is it ? " asks the Most Worshipful.
" It is past 12 o'clock," answers the other.
After several questions and answers of no
lesser depth, a Companion-knock is heard at
the door.  It is our Companion-mason who
presents himself.   He is barefooted, his right
arm naked, also his left breast ; from his right
arm majestically hangs a square ; and round
his waist is a rope going three times around
it ; the end of it is held by the Br .·. *Expert*,
in the rite of the Great Orient of France ; by
Br .·. *Master of Ceremonies*, in the Scotch
rite ; by Br .·. *First Deacon*, in the English
and American Lodges.   In the Misraim rite,
it must be held by the devil himself.   Thus
accoutered, the  Companion knocks at the
door, and a precious scene begins.

" At this noise," says Br .·. *Clavel*, " at this
noise the meeting is moved, and not without
reason ! "   With a faltering voice, Br .·. *First
Overseer* exclaims :   " Most  Worshipful,  a
Companion has  just  knocked  at  the  door."
" See . . . what wants . . . . that Companion," answers, with a truly justifiable emotion,
the Most Worshipful.

Inquiries are made; and, as everything is known in advance, the inquiries are not very complicated. "Why does the Master of Ceremonies come and disturb our grief?" says, with a lugubre tone of voice, the Most Worshipful. "Might not this Companion be one of those miserable whom Heaven delivers up to us for revenge? Br∴ *Expert*, arm yourself and seize upon this Companion. Search him, and ascertain, if there be not on him any trace of his being accessory to the crime which has been committed." This crime is the would-be murder of the Architect Adoniram, put to death by three Companions, whilst he was superintending the works of Solomon's Temple; in reality, it is the punishment inflicted on the Templars, — spiritual ancestors of the Freemasons.

The Expert tears the apron from the Companion, and whilst the latter stands at the door, fraternally guarded by four Brothers armed to the teeth, the Expert goes back to the Most Worshipful, and tells him in a very respectful tone of voice: "Most Worshipful, I have discovered nothing on the Companion indicative of his having committed a murder.

His garments are clean, his hands are pure,
and this apron which I bring to you is stain-
less."

The Most Worshipful feigns not to be convinced. "Venerable Brothers," says he,
" may the surmise which agitates me, etc. .
Should he not be interrogated?" All the
Br . · . bow down their Freemasons' heads in
token of approval; and as the Most Worshipful learns from Br . · . *Expert* that the Companion knows the pass-word, he exclaims,
stricken with amazement: "The pass-word!
. . . . How can he know it? Oh! . . . . It
cannot be but in consequence of his crime."
Forthwith, a new search is made in the
pockets, and all about the Companion who is
all the while there, half-naked, as Marlborough
between his four officers.

During the whole of this, the unfortunate
last received Master is there spending himself in his coffin, and reflects at his ease on
the depth of the Masonic Ceremonies. As it
is somewhat long, probably he has been taking all precautions in advance.

Br . · . *Expert* then searches the Companion. He looks at his right hand: "Good

Gods! What have I seen!" he exclaims with horror, feigning to perceive something. "Speak, you wretched man! Confess your crime. How will you give the pass-word? Who has dared to communicate it to you?" The innocent Companion answers with a perfect composure: "The pass-word? I do not know it. My introductor is to give it for me." Then he is introduced, walking backwards, to the middle of "the Room of the Centre;" and having come near the coffin, he turns round about, and he perceives said coffin with the last received Master who plays the dead.

The Most Worshipful explains to him how they are all busy shedding tears over their most respectable Master Adoniram, wickedly killed by three Companions (about two thousand eight hundred and sixty years ago), and he shows to him the poor last received Master, laid in the coffin. The companion, of course, declares that he has not killed Master Adoniram; and the Most Worshipful, fully satisfied with that justification, commands, as a penance, that he be made "to travel." We know those ridiculous journeys; this one is not unlike the others, except that the four armed Masons fraternally accompany the candidate.

Br . ·. *Expert* follows the traveller, and holds him by the rope's end. Returned from his "travels," the Companion is received Master; he takes the oath kneeling, the two points of an open compass being applied to his breast. He is led "to the West," from where he is led back "to the East;" "it is the mysterious march of the degree of Master."

This mysterious march affords time to the dead Brother noiselessly to creep out of the coffin; and when the new Master comes near to it, it is empty. The Most Worshipful descends from his throne — for he has a throne. Here commences the lamentable reciting of the would-be murder of the respectable Master Adoniram, by the three jealous Companions, Jubelas, Jubelos, and Jubelum; the Most Worshipful stops three times to give Br . ·. *First Overseer* leisure to strike the new Master, as Adoniram was struck by his three murderers; first on the neck, with an iron ruler; then on the heart, with a

square; finally, on the forehead, with a mal
let. After which, two Brothers seize upon
the fictitious Adoniram, and stretch him in
the coffin, as if he were dead. The bystand-
ers simulate looking up their dear Master
Adoniram; after painful researches from the
East to the West, and from the West to the
East, they find him, thanks to the acacia
branch, which indicates to them where lies
his corpse. The Most Worshipful declares
that it is in a state of corruption, and says:
*Mac Benac*, that is the flesh leaves the bones.
(Is not all this quite cheerful and amusing?)
The Most Worshipful drags from the coffin
the would-be dead man, puts on his left
shoulder his own left hand, and tells him in
the right ear: *Mac*, and in the left ear *Benac*,
words which inundate the resuscitated fellow
with lights and consolations. The Brothers,
with their black aprons and their skulls,
lighted by the yellow candle and the skull
transformed into a lantern, break forth in
joyful singing.

The Br . · . New Master renews the oath
"to reveal nothing to inferior Brothers and
to the profane," and they give him the initia-

tion, viz: the Masonic Catechism, and the
Master's Sign.   This sign is made by shutting
four fingers of the right hand, putting the
thumb on the stomach, so as to form an angle,
whilst the back of the left hand is held before
the eyes, the thumb pointing down.   The
Master's Catechism calls that sign "the sign
of horror," because it signifies the horror
with which the Masters were struck when
they perceived Adoniram's corpse.

These gloomy fooleries are the initiation
ceremonial to the third and last degree of
exterior Freemasonry.   This begins to smell
of conspiration and secret society; and one
can understand how easily from that very
large number are drawn recruits for the occult Freemasonry, for the leaders of Secret
Societies.   We shall see of what gross un-
godliness are composed the mysteries which
are then revealed to the new Master.   It is
sheer Materialism.

Therefore can we fearlessly say: no matter
how much they may be duped, the Freema-
sons-Apprentices, Companions, and Masters,
are highly guilty, highly imprudent, and
highly silly.

.

## XI.

### OF THE HIGH DEGREES OF FREEMASONRY.

So are called many initiations, often inde
pendent one from the other, varying accord
ing to places and countries, of which some
are recent, some are extinct. There are Masons, among them most of the heads of exterior Freemasonry, who deny them. Others
acknowledge, praise and join them, yet do
not belong to the occult Freemasonry, or to
the Secret Societies properly so called.

The high degrees are like an efflorescence—
more and more secret and ungodly — of common Freemasonry, an initiation further advanced, though still incomplete, towards
what might be called the soul of Freemasonry, that is, towards the ultimate aim of its
plots. This ultimate aim is universal destruction of all royalty and of all religion:
it is the universal rebellion of the World
against God and against His Christ; it is
Satan and Man who strive to reign over the

world, in the place of God and His Christ.
A part of that infernal Secret has been un-
veiled, and the half-honest Freemasons vainly
deny it.

"The aim of the Order must remain its
first secret," said in 1774 the Grand Lodge of
Germany; "the world is not robust enough to
bear its revelation." Masons themselves,
even those in the high degrees are not deemed
"robust enough;" for, at the initiation to one
of the high degrees of the Scotch rite, the
Master of the Lodge tells the candidate:
"By means of this degree, a thick wall is
raised between us and the profane, *and even
between many of our own* . . . . What you
have learned so far, is nothing compared to
the secrets which shall certainly be revealed
to you in future . . . . *The care we take to
hide them even from our own Brothers*, has
surely given you ideas worthy of the thing[1]
(true Masonic style).

In all the Masonic rites taken together,
there are, it is said, nearly one thousand degrees. In the rite of the Gr ∴ Or ∴ ap-

[1] Admission to the degree of "Senior." From the
Ritual of the Mother Lodge of the Three Globes.

pear thirty-three of them; in the Scotch rite, thirty-three likewise, although but seven are generally conferred; the others are no doubt too sublime, and the eyes might be injured by excess of light. The Misraim rite seems to stop at one hundred degrees; there, doubtless, one enjoys the clearest light.

We should here note that, by God's grace, all the branches of the Masonic tree fraternally detest one another. Their divisions are our salvation. The same is true of Freemasonry as of Protestantism; there is unity of name and of hatred, but endless division between all the sects of *The Sect*. Division is characteristic of the works of Satan, because unity exists only in Truth and in Charity.

The most known among the high degrees seem to be those of "*Judge-Philosopher Grand-Commander-Unknown, Elect, Senior, Knight of St. Andrew, Knight of the Sun, Knight Kadosch, and Rosicrucian.*

## XII.

### OF THE HIGH DEGREE OF JUDGE-PHILOSO-PHER-GRAND-COMMANDER-UNKNOWN.

When received, the *Judge-Philosopher-Grand-Commander-Unknown* is boldly told the true and practical meaning of Adoniram's legend. The words are textually recorded by Br . ·. Ragon in his book on *Masonic Orthodoxy:* " Do not the degrees through which you have passed," says the Master of the Lodge, " induce you to apply our legend of Adoniram's murder, to the tragical and fatal end of James Molay, Judge-Philosopher-Grand-Commander of the Order? *Have you not prepared your heart for vengeance ?* Do you not feel *the implacable hatred* which we have sworn against the three traitors *on whom we must revenge the death of James Molay?* This is, Brother, THE TRUE MASONRY, *such as it has been handed down to us.*"

Practically, those three traitors are : first, the Pope, and, with him, the whole Church, the whole Christendom, the whole religious order; second, the King, and, with him, the whole civil society and all governments; third, the military power, which has taken the place of the old military-religious orders, devoted to the defence of Faith.

The adept is now made to see, but it is as yet only a glimpse — that Atheism, or the worship of the God-nature, is the fundamental doctrine of Freemasonry. "Know how to take your place, is he told, among men whose only doctrine is: Courage and Morals. This doctrine is the rule laid on us by our Constitution." The *courage*, is the blind and savage will which is to lead to undertake any thing, even crime and murder; the *morals*, obedience to nature's instincts. We shall presently see samples of it.

At last they tell him: "Here you are now put *on a level with the zealous Masons who have devoted themselves with us to the common vengeance.* Conceal carefully from the public the high destiny reserved for you . . . . You are now, Brother, one of the elect called *to the accomplishment of the Grand Work.* Amen.

After this *pious* speech, the Master of the

4

Lodge hands to the new Br ∴ Judge-Philosopher-Grand-Commander-Unknown, the insignia of his high degree, and points to him
his special work. The insignia—the *jewel* of
the adept — is a dirk ; his work — vengeance.
Is all this clear ?

## XIII.

### OF THE HIGH DEGREE OF KNIGHT KADOSCH.

I do not know why the Knights Kadosch
are called Knights Kadosch. Their initiation
is highly seasoned with a strong smell of
blood, murder, vengeance, rebellion, and un-
godliness. When Louis Philippe Egalité
(the only one of the Grand-Orients of France
ever admitted into the dark secrets of "the
true Masonry ") was initiated to the degree
of Knight Kadosch, he was made to stretch
on the floor as a dead man, and there, to re-
new all the oaths which he had already taken
in the inferior degrees ; then a dirk was put
in his hand, and he was commanded to go
and strike a crowned manikin, placed in a
corner of the room, near a skeleton. . . . .

Some liquid of a blood-color flew from the wound on the candidate, and covered the pavement. Moreover, he was ordered to cut the head of that manikin, to hold it up in his right hand, and to keep the dirk stained with blood in his left hand; and he did it all. Then he was informed that the bones before him were those of James Molay, Grand-Master of the Order of Templars, and that the man whose blood he had just spilt, and whose bloody head he was holding in his right hand, was Philippe-le-Bel, King of France.[1] It is clear that, Philippe-le-Bel having been dead nearly five hundred years, the oath of murder and vengeance was not directed towards his person, but towards his royalty. Consequently, the new *Kadosch*, as a true *knight*, was one of the foremost among the assassins of Louis the 16th. Almost all of them were Freemasons.

The Masonic Ritual expressly says that the new Elect must avenge the condemnation of James Molay " either figuratively on the au-

1 Montjoie, *History of the Conjuration of Louis Philippe of Orleans Egalité*

thors of his punishment, or implicitly on *who-ever deserves it by right.*"—" Whom do you know?" he is asked.—"Two abominable men."—" Name them."—" Philippe-le-Bel and Bertrand de Goth" (Pope Clement the Vth).

According to Br . · . Ragon "the sacred author," it is not only a crowned manikin, which a Knight Kadosch is now bound to strike on the day of his initiation, it is a serpent with three heads, the first of which wears a tiara and a key, the second a crown, and the third a sword: emblems of Papacy, Royalty, and Military power, which united to destroy the Order of Templars. "This serpent with three heads designates the evil principle," says the same Br . · . Ragon.[1]

The secret of the sect leaks out more and more.

[1] *A Philosophical and Interpretative Treatise on Ancient and Modern Initiations.*

## XIV.

### OF THE HIGH DEGREE OF ROSICRUCIAN.

At the reception of a Rosicrucian, the Chief of the Lodge is no more Venerable nor Most Worshipful; he is called "Most Wise and Perfect Master," and all the officers of the Lodge are "Most Powerful and Perfect." *Perfection* is the distinguishing character of this degree; still let us not confound: it is Masonic Perfection.

The candidate is questioned, among other things, on the meaning of the world-renowned inscription: *Inri*, which was put by Pilate on the Cross of Our Lord Jesus Christ. With Masons, it does not signify any more Jesus of Nazareth, King of the Jews; it means, oh horrible blasphemy! " that the Jew Jesus of Nazareth, was led by the Jew Raphael[1] into Judea, there to be justly punished for his crimes." As soon as the candidate has given

[1] Who is that Jew Raphael ? Could he be, by chance, the traitor Judas, so symphathetic to Br.·. Renan ?

to the "Most Wise" this sacrilegious interpretation, the "Most Wise" exclaims: "Brothers, the word has been found again!" Thus, "the word," the secret of the advanced degrees of Freemasonry, is hatred to Jesus Christ!

In the Masonic legends, Our Lord, as descending from King Solomon, *justly* atones on the Cross for the pretended murder of Adoniram by Solomon, jealous of his architect. Adoniram is the pretended descendant of Cain, the pretended son of Lucifer and Eve; and the actual war of Revolution and Freemasonry against Church and Royalty, is nothing but the fatal and logical consequence of a war begun in the earthly Paradise: the war of Lucifer, of Cain his son, of Adoniram his descendant, and of a whole superior race, which has received the gift of science, of light and of true virtue, against God, Adam, Abel, and Solomon,—against Jesus, and the inferior race of Adam's children, personified by the Priests and the Kings; this latter race's special trait being blind force, tyranny and ignorance. According to Masons, God is jealous of Lucifer and persecutes him; Cain is persecuted by Adam and Abel, &c. It is all topsy-turvy; it is just the reverse of truth; it is the apotheosis of rebellion and the crucifixion of Truth and Righteousness; in a word, it is Revolution, which, in its fundamental doctrine, is essentially antichristian, atheist, satanic.

However much advanced in the knowledge of the *secret* of Masonry may be all the Brothers of the high degrees, we must acknowledge that they have not as yet left "the ill-lighted antechamber," as said "little Tiger;" they are only growing up Masons, all stalks and flowers. The fruit is much, much further hidden in the dark, deep recesses of the Sect. A Priest was saying this, one day, to a sort of honest man, but short-sighted, and long ago promoted to the degree of Rosicrucian. This poor man would see in the Ceremonial of the Lodges nothing but historical mummeries. "He spared no pains," said that Priest, "to impress me more favorably with a society in which he was proud to have held important posts. He decidedly wanted to convert me to Freemasonry. I knew he had but one step more to take to come to the

point when the veil is torn, when it becomes
utterly impossible to deceive oneself about
the ultimate aim of the true adepts. To
convince me, he resolved to take that step.

Very few days after, I see him come to my
house in a state baffling all attempt at descrip-
tion. "Oh! my dear friend, my dear friend,"
exclaimed he, "how right you were! . . Ah!
how right you were! Where was I, O my
God, where was I?" He sat, or rather fell,
down on a chair, able only to repeat: "Where
was I? where was I? . . Ah! how right you
were!" I wished he had given me some of
the particulars of which I was yet ignorant.
He only answered: " *You were right, but it is
all I can say.*" Still, he added that if he accepted what was proposed to him, he could
repair his fortune ruined by the Revolution.
"If I wish," said he, "to set out for London,
Bruxelles, Constantinople, or any other city
that I may choose, neither my wife, nor my
children, nor I, shall ever be in want of anything." "Yes," answered I, "but on condition that you shall go preaching everywhere
equality, liberty, and the whole Revolution!"
—"Just so," murmured he. " But once more,

this is all I can tell you. Ah! my God, where was I ?"[1]

The poor man simply was in the high degrees of exterior Masonry; and he had just been allowed to look under the cards. Let us have our turn, and look at them.

## XV.

### OF THE TRUE FREEMASONRY, WHICH IS OCCULT AND ALL SECRET.

This Freemasonry is not, any more, that of the Lodges; it is not even that of the high degrees; it is purely and simply the Secret Society.

In the back Lodge, the Masons throw off the mask; they scorn and reject the ridiculous and wicked symbolism of the primary initiations; they go straight to the mark: *" War on God, on His Christ, and on His Church! War on Kings, and on all human power which is not with us!"* This is their motto; this is their rallying cry.

[1] The Abbe Barruel: *Jacobinism Unmasked.* Tome 2. pp. 312 and follow.

There, no Grand-Orients, no Grand-Masters, but a frightful unity, realized by an occult government, as plain as it is skilfully organized. "Remember," said lately the wretched Mazzini, "remember that *an association of free and equal men* (always the same formula!) who aim at overturning a country (he might have said all countries) is bound to have a plain, clear and popular organization."[1]

At the head of all this tenebrous army, is one chief, only one and unknown, who stands back in the shade, and who holds all the *Shops* and Lodges in his hand; mysterious and terrible chief to whom are bound, by an oath of blind obedience, all the Masons of all Rites and of all degrees, who do not even know his name, and in whose existence most of whom refuse to believe. This diabolical man is more powerful than any King in this world. In the last century, that chief was, for very many years, an obscure German, named Weishaupt.

The Patriarch of the Secret Societies is known only to four or five picked adepts,

[1] Proclamation of April, 1834.

each one of whom keeps him in relation with
a Section or Lodge (no matter about the
name), and the adepts of that Section know
nothing about the part played among them by
the Lieutenant of the Grand-Chief.   Each
one of the Masons of the Section represents
it in turn, in an inferior section, the members
of which knowing nothing of it; and so forth
down to the most insignificant Lodges of
exterior Freemasonry, down to the Masonic
meetings apparently the most foreign to the
plots of the Secret Societies.

In this *under-masonic* hierarchy, each one
is led without knowing by whom, and fulfills
orders of which the origin and real purpose
are unknown to him.   It is the true, genuine
Secret Society, secret even for those who are
members of it.   About forty years ago, the
Roman police came very near catching the
chief himself of that wide conspiracy.   Car-
dinal Bernetti, Secretary of State under Leo
the 12th, succeeded in seizing upon a part
of the intimate correspondence of the heads
of the Supreme Lodge, that is, of that first
Masonic Lodge under the immediate direction
of the Grand-Chief.   One of those villains

was in the service of the First Secretary of
the Emperor of Austria, Prince Metternich,
who had in him the utmost confidence. His
war-name was *Nubius.* Another was a Jew
whose war-name was "Little Tiger." The
correspondence of a third one indicated a
rich Italian landlord. At that time, the centre of the grand plot was in Italy.

To distinguish it from exterior Freemasonry, the occult one was called *Carbonarism.*
Like Freemasonry, Carbonarism is one and
universal; it is "the militant part of Freemasonry." The number of its adepts is unknown.

Br . · . Louis Blanc, admires, thereby officially proving its existence, the organization
of Carbonarism : "It is," says he, " something
powerful and marvellous." . . . It was agreed
that around a Mother association (what Mother, great Gods !) called the *High Vente,* there
should be formed, under the name of *Central
Ventes,* other associations, under which should
act *Particular Ventes* (the word *Vente* means
meeting). To escape the Penal Code, twenty
was the number of members of each association. The *High Vente* was self-recruiting.

To form the *Central Ventes*, the following mode was adopted: Two members of the *High Vente* would take with them a third person, without trusting him with the knowledge of their own degree, and they would name him *President* of the future *Vente*, appointing themselves, one *Deputy*, the other *Censor* in it. The *Deputy's* office being to correspond with the upper association, and that of *Censor* to control the working·of the secondary one, the *High Vente* thus would be, as it were, the brains of each of the *Ventes* created by it, remaining meanwhile towards it in possession of its own secret and acts . . . . There was in that combination a wonderful elasticity (that of the serpent). Soon the *Ventes* became very numerous.

Br . · . Blanc adds, with the candor of "the terrible child:" "The impossibility of completely eluding the efforts of the Police had been foreseen:[1] to render them of less im-

---

[1] The better to succeed in this, and to draw in military men, the sect had added to the ordinary organization of the *Ventes* a military organization, or, rather, military appellations : *legions, cohorts, centuries, maniples ;* and according to the needs of the time being, presented now one face, now another.

portance, it was agreed that the *Ventes* should
act in common, without however knowing
each other, and in such a way that the Police
could not, except by penetrating into the
*High Vente*, seize upon the whole collective
system of the organization. Consequently,
every *Carbonaro* belonging to a *Vente*, was
forbidden to try to be admitted into another.
*This prohibition was under penalty of death.*

The duties of a *Carbonaro* were: To have
a gun and fifty cartridges (eminently philanthropic precaution); to be ready *to sacrifice
himself* (we know what this means); to blindly obey the orders of unknown chiefs.[1] This
formidable organization, divulged by Br . · .
Louis Blanc, had been combined in the *Lodge
of the Friends of Truth.*

Thus, behind the Lodge is the back Lodge;
behind the Apprentice, Companion, and Master-mason, and even behind the Freemasons
of the high degrees is hidden the *Carbonaro*
Freemason, the man of the Secret Society
and of the *Ventes.* The Lodges which Freemasonry publicly acknowledges hide from all

[1] History of ten years.    Tome 1.

eyes the back Lodges; the degrees hide the back degrees; the avowed doctrine hides the mysterious doctrine; the silly rites and cere· monies hide the occult plots; the ridiculous secrets have been invented the better to hide the true secret; in one word, public Masonry hides secret Masonry.

There is an intimate but occult connection between Freemasonry and Carbonarism; one is the body, the other the soul; one is the army of soldiers, the other the army of chiefs; one is led, the other leads.

Such is guiltless Freemasonry which pre· tends to be slandered by the Church.

## XVI.

### HORRIBLE EXCESSES PRACTISED BY THE MA- SONS OF THE BACK LODGES.

Many of these Sectaries shrink neither from sacrilege nor from assassination. At Rome, during the revolution of 1848, several nightly meetings were broken into, one among others in the suburb called *Transtevere*. in which the adepts, men and women, met to

celebrate what they called " the Mass of the
Devil." Upon an altar decorated with six
black candles, a ciborium was deposited;
each member, after having spit on the Cruci-
fix and trampled it under feet, brought and
put in the Ciborium a consecrated Host,
which he had received in the morning in some
Church, or which he had bought from some
wicked poor old woman for money, like Judas.
Then began, I do not know what diabolical
ceremony, which was concluded by an order
given to all to draw the dirk, to ascend the
altar, and to strike repeated blows at the
Blessed Sacrament. At the end of that Mass,
all lights were put out.

From Italy, these sacrilegious practices
have crept amongst us; and very recently,
they have discovered the existence of a kind
of under-Freemasonry, already fully organized, for the exclusive purpose of agreeing
about the means the more efficaciously and
surely to annihilate Faith. The sect is divided into small sections of twelve or fifteen persons each, no more, lest public attention were
awakened. It is recruited among literary
men, or, at least, among persons, who, by their

social position, talents or fortune, exercise
influence around them. The heads of sections do not reside at the places of meetings,
but in Paris, — which is their headquarters.
Horrible to relate ! each adept, to be enrolled,
must bring, on his initiation day, a consecrated Host, and trample it under feet in presence of the Brothers. I have been assured
that this infernal Sect already exists in most
of the large cities of France. They have
named to me as being beyond all doubt in
the number, Paris, Marseilles, Aix, Avignon,
Lyons, Châlons-sur-Marne and Laval.

The reality of the following fact — which
is after all but the repetition of crimes of the
same nature, frequently perpetrated in Italy,
for twenty years past — has been affirmed to
me, as resting on the testimony of an ear-
witness, a venerable and most credible Priest.

A young man had become a member of
Freemasonry. It seems that he soon was
judged *ripe* for grand deeds. From the
Lodge, he passed to the back Lodge, and one
day he was designated to do away with a
victim of the sect. He was obliged to follow
the individual everywhere, and was not able

5

to strike him but in America. He came back
to France, racked with remorses of conscience, half decided no more to have a share
in *the works* of secret Freemasonry. But soon
a new order was issued; a second murder, a
second vengeance is needed. This time his
heart revolted, and he resolved to take to
flight and thus escape the tyranny of the
dirk.

He therefore secretly left Paris to go *incog-
nito* to Algeria. Hardly was he in Marseilles,
when he received at the hotel in which he
was, a brotherly note running thus: "We
know thy design. Thou shalt not escape us.
Obedience or death!" Terrified, he retraces
his steps, and stops at Lyons in an out-of-the-
way tavern. Half an hour afterwards, an
unknown man brings for him a note couched
about in the same words: "Thou shalt obey,
or die!"

He immediately leaves the tavern and the
city, and penetrated with repentance as well
as with terror, he takes by-ways to seek
shelter in the monastery of la Trappe of
Dombes, near Belley. The day after his ar-
rival, same warning, same threat: "We are

following thee ; in vain thou triest to escape from us."

Finally, bewildered, beside himself, and knowing by experience that the Sect never forgives, he went, by advice of one of the Fathers of la Trappe, to consult the Priest who has related all this, and who found the means, intrusting him to fearless Missionaries, to make the terrible blood-hounds bent on pursuing him, lose his trace.[1]

This frightful fact is but the literal realization of the clear and precise instructions which at present rule the Sect; here are

[1] Very recently, the daughter of a Freemason, by an innocent indiscretion, confirmed the reality of those stern, inexorable proceedings. That child, twelve years old, had often heard her Father speak of Freemasonry and declare that he was a member of it.

Thanks to her good mother's influence, she was put as a boarder in an academy conducted by Religious ; and she more than once repeated before her companions, and before the Sisters and the Chaplain of the Institution, those words which fell from the lips of her Father : "If any one of us betrays the secret confided to him in Freemasonry, he shall be pursued to the end of the world ; and he shall be done away with, without the Police, or any human being, ever being able to know what has become of him."

some of the articles of this occult constitution,
framed by Mazzini :

"ART. 30th. Those who will not obey the orders
of the Secret Society, or who would reveal its mysteries, shall be unmercifully stabbed to death. Same
punishment for traitors."

"ART. 31st. The secret tribunal shall pass sentence,
and designate one or two members to carry it out immediately."

"ART. 32d. Whoever will refuse to carry out the
sentence, shall be considered a perjurer, and, as such,
killed forthwith."

"ART. 33d. If the guilty man escapes, he shall be
pursued without intermission, and everywhere; and
he must be struck by an invisible hand, were he even
on his mother's bosom, or in the tabernacle of Christ!"

Well, after all this, go and be a Freemason!


## XVII.

WHAT THE BROTHERS OF THE BACK LODGES
THINK AND SAY OF, AND EXPECT TO DO
WITH, THEIR DEAR BROTHERS OF THE EX-
TERIOR LODGES.

Let us learn it from themselves: "The
Lodges," says the famous "Little Tiger,"
" can now-a-days create gluttons; they never

will give birth to *citizens*. There are too
many dinners given by the T.·.C.·.and the
T.·.R.·. Br.·. of all the Orients; but it is *a
"depot," a sort of " stud," a centre through which
one must pass before he may come to us* . . . .
There is too much of the pastoral and gas-
tronomic in it, but it has *a purpose which is
to be always encouraged.* When you teach a
man to hold up his tumbler at the word of
command, you obtain the mastery over his
will, intellect and liberty (but then, what becomes of the " freemen, the *Free*masons ? ").
You have him at the end of your fingers ; you
go round him, you study him. You divine
his tastes, inclinations and tendencies ; *when
he is ripe for us,* you lead him towards the
Secret Society, of which exterior Freemasonry cannot any more be but the tolerably ill-
lighted antechamber." [1]   Truly, we are betrayed only by our own people !

A Freemason who in good faith disclaims
all idea of affiliation to Secret Societies, is
then merely a simple Mason, *not as yet ripe.*
He is a kind of honest fellow " who is turned

[1] Letter to the Piedmontese Lodge, Jan. 18th, 1822.

round " to be done up before the sacred **fire.**
No doubt it is highly honorable for him to refuse to be done up, to be unable *to get ripe;* he
is not, however, the less in the hands of the
back Lodges ; and will he, nill he, at the **first**
sign, he must go or die.

Go then into the "depot." Select **your**
place in the " stud." Go and learn " to hold
up arms " with your tumbler! Poor dupes !
I have shown you the bloody precipices on
the brink of which you are made to sing and
eat !

## XVIII.

### How the Masons of the Back Lodges Make Use of and Manage the Princes and Noblemen who Join Freemasonry.

Let them once more speak themselves ; and,
once more let us understand the fatal union
which exists between the exterior and the
occult Freemasonry.

Here are the words, concerning the Princes
Freemasons, in which is couched one of the
secret notes found by the Roman Police under

Leo the XIIth. "There is some good in the citizen, but much more in the Prince. The "*High Vente*" wishes that, under this or that pretext, as many Princes and rich people as possible be introduced into the Masonic Lodges. There are many of them, in Italy and elsewhere, who covet the modest enough honors of the symbolical apron and trowel. Flatter those men who are so fond of popularity; lay hold of them for Freemasonry; the "*High Vente*" will later see what can be made of them for the cause of progress. A Prince who is not heir to a kingdom, is a good chance for us. There are many of them in that case! Make Freemasons of them; *they will answer like glue to catch the simpletons, the intriguers, the fops, the needy.* Those poor Princes are the thing for us, whilst they fancy that they are working for themselves. *They are a splendid signboard.*[1]

They are more than a signboard; they afford a very efficacious protection. Masons themselves say so: "The joining our Order by Princes is a very good omen," says Br·.

---

[1] Letter to the Piedmontese Lodge.

Jeder in his *History of Freemasonry* (p. 149). "Although they cannot contribute to the construction of the Masonic Temple, although we must submit to see the brilliant insignia attached to their button-holes, *they are of a very great value to the Order, on account either of their riches, or of their immense influence.* No matter how free secret associations may appear to be, still, they depend too much on the dispositions of superior classes ; they cannot come to their full growth but in the rays of the sun, under a cloudless sky. Where the Prince frowns, it would look badly did we wish to rise too high, *whilst we may unfurl all sails, when a favorable breeze blows from the Court.* May our august guests continue to remain *dumb and inactive like Martin's doll !* "

Impossible to laugh at people more *freely.*

The " poor Princes " the great men, the rich have allowed themselves to be entrapped. " Thanks to the clever mechanism of the Institution, Freemasonry found Princes and Noblemen to be rather protectors than enemies. Some Kings, as the great Frederic, were pleased to handle the trowel and gird the apron. Why not? *The existence of the high degrees being carefully hidden from them, they knew of Freemasonry only what could be shown without danger.* They had no occasion to think of those degrees, *kept as they were in the lower ones,* where they saw but an opportunity for amusement, merry banquets, principles left and adopted again at the threshold of the Lodges, formulas without any bearing on ordinary life; in a word, a comedy of equality. But, in these matters, tragedy comes on the heels of comedy; and Princes and Noblemen were made *to cover with their name, and blindly to help with their influence occult undertakings directed against themselves.* This fact is attested by another Mason.[1]

We find, besides, in the Scotch Ritual, the form of oath by which Masters bind themselves to hide even from their Grand-Orients, what these must be ignorant of: " I swear and promise never to reveal the least part of our mysteries to any one, *not even to the Master of the whole Order,* the moment I shall see him not acknowledged in a High Lodge."

[1] Br∴. Louis Blanc's *History of the French Revolution.* Tome 2d. pp. 82 and 83.

It goes of itself that (except Philippe Egalité) no Sovereign, no official person joining
Freemasonry, ever has been, is, or shall be
"acknowledged by the High Lodges."  In
the list of the Grand-Masters or protectors
of the Order, we read the names of Louis de
Bourbon, royal Prince (1743); of Marquis of
Larochefoucauld (1777); of Duke of Luxembourg (1784); of Joseph Bonaparte, King of
Spain (1805); of Prince Cambacérès (1807);
of Duke of Choiseul (1827); of Duke Deca-
zes, King Louis Philippe, Lord Palmerston,
Leopold I., King of the Belgians, Prince
Lucien Murat, Count Cavour, &c.  The *Masonic Annuary* indicates among the actual
Grand-Masters, George the Vth., King of Han-
over, the King of Sweden, the Grand-Duke
of Hesse Darmstadt, Prince Frederic of the
Netherlands, and the Grand-Duke of Hesse.
The King of Prussia is the protector of all
the German Freemasons.

Those "august guests" of Freemasonry
know it less than any one else.  From them
its true aim and spirit are most carefully
hidden.  They know its statutes; but those
statutes are framed only to deceive the dupes

who fancy themselves initiated, and above all to ward off public authority. By protecting Freemasonry, the Mason-Princes evidently imagine they protect a good thing, and especially themselves.

Sometimes, however, suspicion goes up to them, and they threaten to suppress the Order; but their uneasiness is easily quieted. " It has at times happened," says Br.·. Ragon, "that persons delegated to suspend, in the name of the Sovereign, Freemasonry in his kingdom, presenting themselves on a Masonic *working* or Feast Day, were blandly received by the officers of the Lodge, and told in a tone of candor: " Come, hear and judge." Were they initiated to a degree of *Elect*, or *Kadosch*, or *Rosicrucian? No, no, indeed !* . . They were admitted to the degree of Apprentice ; they would fraternize with the Masons, and, *on the strength of their report, the order of suspension was revoked.*"[1]

In sober reality, here is the fate reserved for Princes and Noblemen by Freemasonry — the true Freemasonry — when the strongest:

[1] *Philosophical and Interpretative Treatise on the Ancient and Modern Initiations.* p. 44.

" Princes, bigots and Noblemen, the implacable enemies of mankind, *must be annihilated*
(nothing short of that), and their property
assigned to those who, by their talents, science
and virtue, (i. e. to us Masons) *alone* have
the right and power to govern others (and
what of equality? and of liberty?).   Against
those enemies of mankind, *we have all rights,
and all duties.   Yea, everything is lawful to
annihilate them : violence and craftiness, fire
and sword, poison and dagger ; the aim sancti-
fies the means.*"[1]

Therefore, Freemasonry loves Princes, Noblemen and rich men, as  the  wolf loves the
sheep.   Therefore,  Princes,  Noblemen, and
rich men, affiliated to Masonry, far from seeing into the back Lodges, do not even see into the public ones ;  they are seen, and, above
all, shown and paraded in them ;  they are put
in front, as " magnificent  signboards " to bring
in customers.   Did they listen to the Church,
they would not be caught in the trap.

[1] Br . ·. Fichte, Member of the German and Universal Masonry.   *Supplementary Advertisement.*   p. 45.

## XIX.

### OF THE PUBLIC ORGANIZATION OF EXTERIOR FREEMASONRY.

That organization has no connection whatever with that of the occult Freemasonry. Carbonarism or occult Freemasonry is essentially one and universal; it has but one chief; and that chief it does not know. Exterior Freemasonry is one and universal only in its inmost being;— in its form it is multiple. There are about sixty different forms of Freemasonry assuming different names. Thus, there are: the *Grand-Orient* of France, the Gr.∴. O.∴. of Italy, the Gr.∴. Or.∴. of Spain, of Portugal, of the Netherlands, of Saxe, of Mexico, of New Grenada, of Peru, of Hayti, of Brazil, of the United States, &c.; there are the *Grand-Lodges* of Munster, of Scotland, of Denmark, of Hamburgh, of Ireland, of New York, &c.; there are the Scotch "Supreme Council" of France, the Supr.∴. Conc.∴. of the Grand-Duchy of Luxembourg,

of England, of Charleston, of New York, of
Brazil, &c.,— the Swiss Supreme Directory,
the *Oriental* of Misraim, etc., etc.

To speak only of the Gr.·. Or.·. of France,
let us say that the Grand-Master, who goes
by the name itself of Great-Orient, has under
his obedience the Lodges and Workshops of
all the Masons who do not acknowledge either
the Scotch or the Misraim rites. He is assisted
by a large number of counsellors, almost all
of them known and influential persons, among
whom shines the too famous Renan, the daring blasphemer of Christianity; he is Grand-
Chancellor. The Lodges and Workshops are
divided into Provinces or Orients. The decrees of the Grand-Orient thus reach all the
Brothers in a hierarchical way.

But, let it be well noticed, this is only the
Exterior Freemasonry, which does not con-
spire and plot like the other. Moreover, if,
among the high dignitaries of the Order, some
are initiated to the odious mysteries of Carbonarism, it is without the knowledge of authority.

Most of the Lodges have incredible names.
In the " *Universal Annuary of the French*

*and Foreign Freemasonry*, printed at Châlons Sur-Marne, and published in Paris, at Br . · . Pinon's, we find a lengthy enumeration of all those Workshops, all those Lodges with the names and addresses of the Venerables. and of the dignitaries high and low: Br . · . First Overseers, Br . · . Introductors, Br . · . Masters of Ceremonies, Br . · . Sacrificers, Br . · . Orators, Br . · . Masters of Banquets, &c. There are also the names and addresses of the Knights Kadosch, Rosicrucians, of St. Andrew, of the Sun, &c., with the exception, however, of few whom prudence has left in the shade, among others, the name of Renan.

In Paris, and its liberties, there are *seventy-one* Lodges grouped into four Sections, and almost all of them meeting once a month on fixed days, indicated in *the Annuary*.

At those meetings take place the celebrated love-feasts, the brotherly banquets, which in the ideas of the public are all that constitutes Freemasonry. There also are taken up collections in behalf of poor members. Freemasonry highly extols its philanthropy, a colorless caricature of true Charity. The Church alone knows how properly to love the poor.

In the other parts of France, there are *two hundred and five* Lodges ; in Algeria and the Colonies, *twenty-eight ;* in all, *three hundred and four* Lodges, which work under that one Obedience, to the Glory of the Great Architect and for the salvation of souls. The Gr.·. Or.·. of France is at the head, besides, of *thirty-four* Lodges in foreign countries.

Here are some names of Lodges which, reader, may please you much: The Lodge of *Admirers of the Universe, Zealous Philanthropists, St. Anthony of Perfect Contentedness, Triumphing Friends, Cosmopolitan Clement Friendship, Disciples of Memphis, Rose of Perfect Silence, Philosophical Bee-hive, Trinosophists of Bercy*, &c. The other cities have not a less dainty share, and in them blossom the Lodges of *Candor, Love Valley, Simplicity-Constancy, School of Virtue, United Virtues*, &c.

The Scotch and Misraim Rites christen their Lodges with somewhat less ridiculous names. The Scotch rite numbered, in 1866, *ninety-eight* Lodges: *thirty-four* in Paris, *forty-three* in the other cities of France, *twenty-one* in

Algeria and other foreign parts. The Misraim rite seems less prosperous, at least according to the *Annuary* under our eyes.

All the rites of exterior Freemasonry form, I repeat it, but one Masonry; and in the *Annuary*, we see the list of the delegates of all these Obediences to the Supreme Council of the Grand-Orient of France, and to that of the Scotch rite; and it is evident that all the Freemasonries of the whole Universe thus correspond direct one with the other. It is an immense woof filled up by chained and interchained threads, although distinct and often at war.

"Spread all over the world," says the Ritual, "our Brothers nevertheless form but one community. All are initiated to the same secrets, follow the same way, are trained under the same rule, are inspired by the same spirit.[1] No matter to what acknowledged rite a Mason may belong, he is Br . ·. of all the Masons of the world." [2]

---

[1] Degree of Ancient.

[2] General Regulations of Scotch Masonry. Art. 2.

## XX.

### DOES MASONRY LOVE THE POOR AS IT WOULD HAVE US BELIEVE?

We have just spoken of collections and philanthropy: in fact Masonry has succeeded in being everywhere considered as a charitable, good, eminently beneficent and philanthropic Institution. The Church calls herself the mother of the poor. I, exclaims Masonry at every turn, I am their mother.—Does it tell the truth?

It is truthful in this no more than in any thing else; and when it speaks openly, it throws out, on the subject of the poor, revolting acknowledgments. Br∴ Ragon, who gives us an insight into the genuine Masonic spirit, calls the indigent Masons "that *hideous leprosy* of Masonry in France ; "[1] and he warmly recommends to all the Lodges the rule of

---

[1] *Philosophical and Interpretative Treatise on Ancient and Modern Initiations.* pp. 368.

charity laid down by Br.·. Beurnonville:
"Never bring for admission but men who can
stretch out the hand to give, not to beg."

Another Brother, himself an authority,
Br.·. Bazot, speaks of the poor with a no
less Evangelical feeling: "The indigent Mason," says he, "is at your house, on your
heels, in your Lodges always; he is *an evil
genius*, besetting you everywhere and at
all hours. Nothing can make you shake off
his importunity; and his insolence knows no
limits, no obstacles. He is there at your rising, at your business hours, at your meals, at
your going out. It were better to meet him
armed with a dirk; you might at least show
courage against the murdering weapon. Pro-
tected only by his title of Mason, he tells you:
'I am a Mason; give me alms; for I am
your Brother, and your law commands you to
assist those in need. Give, or else I shall
everywhere publish that you are a wicked,
bad Brother.'"

"Give, Masons!" continues the *good*
Brother, "but be ready to give unceasingly.
*The ambush* is permanently set up." (The
ambush! what word! how cynical!)

" The fault lies at the door of the Lodges.
Did Lodges receive in the brotherly (!) association none but honorable men (thus, to be
*honorable,* one must be rich), enjoying an independent position through their fortune or
their industry, they, and all the Masons would
have to alleviate none but transitory misfor-
tunes."[1]  This they call cordial love of the
poor; there is their true, genuine fraternity !
Poor philanthropy ! thou mayest order collections and give away money ; thou art not
even the shadow of Charity ; thou hast no
heart !

## XXI.

### That Freemasonry is a Formidable Power.

Its organization, both occult and public, is
alone sufficient to prove it to evidence.  Its
works likewise prove it ; it boasts, by the in
discreet pen of its most fervent adepts, of
having been, for more than a century, the
unknown, but real cause of all the great religious commotions which have terrified the
whole world, and especially Europe.

[1] Code of the Freemasons. pp. 176 and 177.

It boasts, with proofs at hand, of having given birth to the revolutionary philosophy of the last century, and of having had for its organs Voltaire, Helvetius,[1] Rousseau, Diderot, d'Alembert, Condorcet, Mirabeau, Sieyès, la Fayette, Camille Desmoulins, Danton, Robespierre, Marat, Santerre, Pétion, etc. It boasts of having stricken with a deadly blow Christian Monarchy in the persons of the unfortunate Louis the XVIth, and of Queen Marie Antoinette; it boasts of having brought about in France the bloody revolution of '89 and '93. "When, *from the inmost recesses of*

[1] At the death of Helvetius, the materialist and atheist, his widow sent back his regalia to the *Lodge of the Nine Sisters* to which he had belonged. Helvetius' apron was offered to Voltaire; and Voltaire, the great Voltaire, before girding it, *religiously* kissed it as a relic. Voltaire, who surnamed himself *Christ-mocking*, was not contented with having been received a Freemason in England; his conscience and piety were not satisfied until he was initiated to the French Masonry. He was admitted to it on the 7th of April, 1778, seven weeks before his death, no doubt by way of immediate preparation for it. He was proclaimed Perfect Mason at once, and dispensed with *probations;* "for," said the Brothers, " sixty years of life devoted to virtue and to genius, had made him sufficiently known."

*the Lodges,*" said Br∴ Brémond to the Or∴ of Marseilles, " when, *from the inmost recesses of the Lodges*, went forth those three words: LIBERTY, EQUALITY, FRATERNITY, the Revolution was consummated." And another Mason, initiated from youth to the highest degrees of the Sect, in Prussia, Count of Taugwitz, made in 1822 the following declaration: " I have come to the clear conviction that the drama commenced in 1788 and 1789, the Regicide with all its horrors, not only *had been resolved upon in the Lodges, but were, moreover, the result of associations and oaths.*" Finally, the Grand Chapter of the German Masons, rejoicing to see the havoc caused by infidelity and revolt, already spreading from France over all Europe, and even America, triumphantly exclaimed in 1794: " Our Order has revolutionized the Nations of Europe for many generations to come."

Most of the revolutionary men, so deeply impious, in 1830, were Freemasons. So it was in 1848; only, the antichristian side of the question craftily was much more concealed than in the preceding upturnings.

Nearly all the coryphei of cotemporary impiety are Freemasons : Mazzini, Garibaldi, Kossuth, Juarez, &c. Consequently Freemasonry loudly proclaims that it prepares and puts to execution in the dark, the destruction of the Catholic Religion in Italy, Germany, Austria, Belgium, Spain, Portugal, Mexico. It everywhere fills the most important offices ; it penetrates in all the armies, and great corporations of the State ; it controls most of the newspapers. It gives impulsion at will to most of Governments, and its universal watchword is : "Down with the Church ! Down with authority ! No more Priests ! no more Christ ! no more God !" Let it be well known, this is what Freemasonry means by that magical word *Liberty*, which it makes to glitter before the deceived eyes of all Nations,—as of old, Eden's serpent showed to Eve the beauty of the forbidden fruit.

Freemasonry declares itself to be on the high road to progress and full prosperity. It very recently said through one of its periodical publications : "Unmistakable symptoms prove that the day is dawning when Masonry is to witness a considerable development of its power and influence on the world. More

and more every day does Masonry understand
the importance of its Mission; it is throwing
away the swaddling clothes with which ne-
cessities of a by-gone period had wrapped it.
It knows what its motto means; and soon,
putting aside the last veils of a vague mysti-
cism, it shall proclaim forth as principle and
basis of the Institution, *the complete indepen-
dence of conscience.* Let us rejoice at the suc-
cess of our Brethren's efforts; everywhere
appears the luminous sign of the Eternal
Jehovah." [1]

Who is that " Eternal Jehovah" whose sign
appears everywhere, thanks to the Freemasons? We are going to see it.

## XXII.

THAT FREEMASONRY IS, IN SPITE OF ITS SAY-
INGS, ESSENTIALLY IMPIOUS, ANTICHRISTIAN
AND ATHEIST.

Let no one be deceived; the God whom it
affects to venerate under the whimsical name
of Great Architect of all the worlds, is not

[1] *The Masonic World*, Aug., 1866, and Feb., 1867.

the living God, the only true God, Father,
Son, and Holy Ghost, whom we adore; he is
not our Creator, Lord and Saviour Jesus
Christ, God made man, the only true God;
he is the God of Voltaire, the Supreme Being
of Rousseau, of the Convention, and of Robespierre; he is the God of the Theophilanthro-
pists, the God of the indifferent, sung by
Béranger, the God of Renan and Garibaldi,
the God of the religion of the so-called honest man. He is the God who does not exist.
For that reason, Masons affect to count for
nothing, Revelation or Christ's coming; they
reject the Christian era, and in all their publications they date the years from the Creation;
according to the Christian era, we are (at the
time when I am writing this work) in the
year 1867,—according to the Masonic era,
in 5867. This negation of Christianity were
childish, if it were not impious.

Freemasonry speaks of God solely not to
scare the multitudes. To that same intent, it
traitorously puts on the appearances of a Religion: it has a whole code of ceremonies and
rites; it confers a baptism of its own; it has
a Masonic marriage, a ceremonial for burials,

etc., all of them with invocations, blessings, the use of incense, consecrations,[1] in a word, an appearance of worship. This is for the multitudes.

But, as to your pure-blooded, true Masons, they are not so particular; they openly deny God's existence. The others, those who are not *ripe*, often preserve, with God's name, that vague religious feeling, which does not perplex conscience, and which excites the true Mason's pity. Every one knows that, practically, Deism resembles Atheism in all; it is a respectful and latent Atheism. Now, Freemasonry is Deist in that sense, when it is not avowedly Atheist. For that reason, the German Lodges very recently máde the following declaration: "Deist Freemasons are *above* religious dissensions. We must place ourselves not only above the different Religions, but above all belief in a God of any kind."[2]

In France, they speak as in Germany. It is the heart's outpouring. The *Masonic World* said, when discussing the first article

---

[1] See the *Masonic Ritual.*
[2] *Freemason's Gazette,* Dec 15th, 1866.

of the statutes of Freemasonry, where God's existence and the soul's immortality are mentioned: "What, will some one say, is there nothing required from a man to be worthy to be a Mason? Nothing, except he be an upright man.—Does he reject the idea of God? Suggest to him any idea that may satisfy his reason.—Does he doubt future life? Prove to him that to believe in nothing is an absurdity.—Does he refuse to admit the basis of good morals? *What of that!* if he does live and act as if he admitted them." [1]

Therefore, Freemasonry, Deist or Atheist, is the absolute negation of religion. This is not my saying; it is Proudhon's. Says he: " Freemasonry is *the negation even of the religious element.*" It wants God or Religion no more; it wants to exclude them from education, from private and public morals, from man's life and death. Its most serious writers, especially the modern ones, are at the head of the hideous movement of atheism and materialism, which has been felt for some years; they praise and endorse with complacency

[1] *Freemason's Gazette,* September, 1866.

the most daring antichristian publications, such as *the Independent Ethics, the Free Thought, the Free Conscience, the Solidarity* newspapers. "We welcome," lately said a Freemason newspaper, "all our new co-writers, some of them are old friends, and *we are happy to know that all these newspapers, not one excepted, are controlled by Masons,* and that *the majority of the writers are Masons.*"[1]

In Belgium and everywhere, Freemasonry gives birth to that awful Sect of the *Solidaires,* so called because they bind themselves "in solido," by an express contract, one to the other, to live without religion and to die without any of its last rites,—like dogs.

That this or that Freemason does not go to that excess of irreligion, we readily grant; but, as to Freemasonry in itself, it may say what it pleases, it is an essentially impious, antichristian and atheist Institution.

[1] *The Masonic World,* November. 1866.

## XXIII.

### How Masonry Finds its Happiness in the Worship of the Sun.

Yes, of the Sun, the Moon, and the Stars.

It is in the name of Science, and intellectual progress, of which it forever speaks, that Freemasonry pretends that "God is neither proved, nor provable;" that the Christian ethics, which rest on the fear and love of God, are childish, useless and immoral; that our Lord either never did exist, or was just a man like any other; time, it says, has come when we must be done with the Church, the Pope and the Priests. And, strange to say! through its pretended science and intellectual progress, it comes to an excess of stupidity which would be incredible, were it not attested by its own adepts: do you know who is, at bottom, the God to whom it looks? . . . The Sun! Yes, once more, the Sun; as do those brutes with a human face met with at times in the lowest and most degraded strata of our unchristian society. Listen, if you doubt.

In the initiation ceremony to the degree of Master, the third in Freemasonry, here is what the " Most Worshipful " says point blank to the new elect: " The Adoniram of Freemasonry, the same as Osiris, Mithra, Bacchus, and all the gods worshipped in ancient mysteries; *is one of the thousand personifications of the Sun.* Adoniram, in fact, means in Hebrew lofty life, which clearly designates the position of the Sun in relation to the Earth.

. . . In all ceremonies performed in Lodges, *you will constantly trace the same idea.* Thus, our association has put itself under the invocation of St. John, *that is, of Janus, the Sun of the Solstices.* We, consequently, at the two Solstices of the year (June 21st and December 21st) celebrate *the feast of our Patron,* with full (g)astronomical ceremonies. The table at which we sit, is in the shape of a horseshoe, and figures the half of the circle of the Zodiac ; and in *our works at table* (sic) we offer seven toasts in honor of the seven planets."

Br.·. Rebold says that the miracles and

the acts of the life of Jesus must be explained by "*solar* appearances." Br.∴. Grand-
Chancellor Renan declares, in the *Revue des
deux-Mondes* (Oct. 15th, 1863,) that "*the worship of the Sun is the only rational and scien-
tific worship*," and that "*the Sun is the special God of our Planet!*"—Textual quotation.

The worship of the Sun! here, then, is the
last word of those *strong-minded men*, who
speak of nothing but progress, light, science,
and who modestly denominate themselves
"Sublime Princes of Truth!" Here is the
*pious* meaning of that Gospel according to
St. John, which we have seen placed before
the eyes of the yet profane man, at the beginning of the Apprentice's trials! Here is the
famous "light," here are "the purifying
flames" which the Venerable generously
gives to the Apprentice! Here is the meaning of "the glittering star," and of the blue
ribbon put on across from shoulder to side!
The worship of the Sun, the degrading worship of matter, of the God-nature, or, to speak
more correctly, an atheism the more shameful
because it hides itself under the cloak of morality and beneficence, and which is not only

impious, but moreover, hypocritical: what a
punishment for the pride of those strong-
minded men!

And Freemasonry dares to call itself "the
origin and spring of all the social virtues"
(words of Br.·. Ragon), and also " the purest
philosophy, the origin of the fables of all worships (sic), the well in which Truth seems to
have taken refuge!!!" What impudence!

From that dark well have sprung up, in
fact, for nearly two centuries, the waves of
blasphemies, ungodly acts, daring negations,
lies, slanders against the Church. rebellions,
destructions, occultly atheist institutions,
which threaten Christian civilization with to-
tal shipwreck! From that well have especially sprung up in these latter years, Renan's
and Proudhon's blasphemies — diabolical blasphemies which Lodges have scattered to the
winds in all languages. From that well, spring
up daily the powers of all sorts which rush
against Rome, shake off the foundations of
the Papacy, and which would fain uncrown
Christ and His Vicar.

At bottom, materialism is the doctrine of
Freemasons.

## XXIV.

### THE MASONIC PRESS.

Masonry displays a feverish activity in its propagandism; peaceful zeal is truth's characteristic — agitation, error's. Masonry agitates itself prodigiously. Its means of action are varied and powerful; it fires at us on all sides. Let us prove it, although confining ourselves to France.

Its first weapon is "the Press." Already we have seen that most newspapers are under its indirect control. It has, besides, publications of its own, more or less wicked, according to their greater or lesser frankness. It has first *The Freemason*, a monthly review, quite anodyne, established in 1847, on the eve of the February revolution, and destined to *enlighten* the mind and to make joyful the heart of all the *green* Br. ·.. It is *respectful* towards Religion, at least in its deportment; it is the orthodox and mystic paper of Freema-

7

sonry. The genuine *progress-Masons* unmercifully call it "Jesuit."

Next it has *the Journal of the Initiated*, also a monthly review, published in two similar parts, the latter of which is called *the new Birth*. In this one neither the name of Freemason nor of Freemasonry is pronounced; it is "the part of propagandism; *it propagates the work of Freemasonry without naming it, in order to keep away prejudices.*"[1]  O good faith! O candor!

It has *the Masonic World*, much more *advanced* publication, and, of course, much more *frank* and more *Masonic*. We have heretofore quoted it several times. It wages war on the two others, and accuses them to be behind the times, and form-serving; as to itself, it is squarely a free-thinking, independent paper, far above all religious ideas. It is the liberal camp, which aims at reforming exterior Freemasonry, and at officially suppressing even the name of "Great Architect of the Universe." That party is rapidly progressing despite of its failure in having yet

[1] No. for January, 1867.

its views adopted. Although most of the
*Jesuit* Masons look upon this traditional formula only as a mere formality, which leaves
to all the Brothers full liberty to be atheists,
nevertheless, the *liberal* Masons cling to its
suppression; this old thing smells too much
of Religion, and may have its dangers.

Masonry also claims as its own the fully
atheist newspapers above-mentioned: *The
Independent Ethics, the Free Thought, the Free
Conscience, the Solidarity;* and there is nothing to prevent it from counting amongst its
most genuine productions, or at least, among
its most devoted auxiliaries, a good number
of large and small newspapers, such as *the
Siècle, the National Opinion, the National Future, the Times, the Liberty, the Journal des
Débats.* Those papers do not, however, feel
it necessary to date their numbers from the
year 5867. They likewise discreetly leave in
the shade the slang of the Brothers and
friends, as well as the celebrated sacramental
sign. · ..

The *Revue des deux Mondes* is, under
that same point of view, in the service of
Freemasonry and its sacrilegious work. Near-

ly all its contributors are known rationalists, or heretics; some are atheists, like Renan, Taine, Littré, &c.

Thus, in France, the Press is mostly Masonic, that is, anticatholic and antichristian. What a danger for the Faith of the people !


## XXV.

### THAT FREEMASONRY IS BEGINNING TO LAY HOLD ON YOUTH BY MEANS OF INSTRUCTION AND EDUCATION.

This second weapon is perhaps more dangerous even than the first. Masonry seemed to have somewhat neglected it; it sees it, and is concocting projects which we will presently unveil.

By Baptism, by Catechism, and by First Communion, the Church makes Christians, and lays the basis of their religious life. Freemasonry, which is the anti-Church, rejects all that, or to speak more correctly, wants to lay, in place of this Christian basis, a Masonic one, completely estranged from Christianity.

It first tries to put the Masonic seal on quite young children. It has a ceremony of adoption which is performed "under the shining of the Masonic light," and it says to the poor child whom it adopts: "May the Masonic light shine before your eyes, as later we shall make it shine before your mind." [1]  As the baptized child becomes a Christian and a member of the Church, so the *adopted* child becomes a *young wolf*, if a male; a *she young wolf*, if a female,— and member of Freemasonry. These *young wolves*, if indigent, are entitled to the Brothers' alms.

In a hospital at Avignon, a poor woman lately came to the Sisters with a babe eleven months old; she told the Superioress that she was passing through the city, and came to ask some medicine for her child. The Religious, whilst fondling it, saw a strange medal hanging from its neck. " What medal is this ? " said she. " It is the Freemason's medal," answered the poor woman; and as the Sister was blaming her for it, warning her that Free-

[1] Br.·. Ragon, *Ritual of the Adoption of Young Wolves.*

masons are excommunicated, the unfortunate woman frankly answered: "If I present myself with this medal before the Chief of a Lodge, I shall immediately obtain from him money to enable me to continue my journey."

It seems that in certain wards of Paris, the number of *young wolves* is very large, among the children of the laboring classes. Unfortunate little ones!

But it is, above all, through schools that Freemasonry seeks to lay hold on the children. "The world of profane people must be prepared to receive *our principles*," said "*the Masonic World*," Oct., 5866. "I consider primary instruction as the corner stone of our edifice . . Must religious instruction be taken away from the programme? . . . The principle of supernatural authority (that is, Faith) *which strips man of his dignity, is useless to train children* (what absence of practical good sense!), *and apt to lead them to forsake all morality* (what absence of moral sense!), *therefore, it is urgent to give it up.* We shall teach rights and duties in the name of liberty, of conscience, of reason, and also in the name of solidarity." Is not this a fine specimen of the revolutionary slang, hollow yet sonorous, which, with its high-sounding words, does not know what it says! "Masonry must be the mould of modern Society; it must form *free* men (we know that freedom). To create schools, for adults especially, and orphan asylums, *is the best means to spread Freemasonry.*"

These wishes, adopted by a large number of Lodges, were sanctioned and carried out by a decree from the Grand-Orient of France (in January, 5867, or to use the Christian date, 1867). This decree states "that it was in Council decided that the Gr∴ Or∴ should head a work, the object of which is to encourage and propagate primary instruction, by awarding rewards every year, both to male and female teachers, and to pupils, and by creating, when circumstances shall allow it, primary and adult schools." Then the circular sets forth the organization of the work, which shall be directed by the Lodges, or by committees appointed by them,—the mode of subscribing, and the necessity of showing zeal, with the clause that the rewards and the savings'-banks'-books shall be accompanied by a medal, with the following inscrip-

tion: " Grand-Orient of France. Encourage-
ment to primary instruction given in the name
of the Masons of the Orient of . . . ."

The propagandism of the Protestant schools
is assuredly very dangerous; but this, if I
am not mistaken, will be far, far more.

To bring this to completion, *the Masonic
World* (January, 5867) announces " the composition of a *Catechism of Ethics*, for the use
of children, adapted to their capacity; a catechism which is to teach them to follow their
conscience, rather than tradition (that is rather than Religion and the Church), to be virtuous on principles (as if Christians were not
virtuous on principles!), on conviction (as if
Faith was not a conviction the most serious
of all, and even the only serious one!), and
disinterestedly (as if hope of heaven and
fear of hell prevented us from serving and
loving God purely!)." In the month of June,
1867, a reward of *five hundred francs* was to
be and surely has been given to that effect.

Finally, in November, 1866, *a league of instruction* for France, in imitation of the one
at work in Belgium since 1864, was inaugur-
ated by the Masons of Alsace.   That league's

fundamental principle is "to subserve the
private interests *of no religious denomination
whatsoever*," in other words, altogether to ban-
ish Faith from instruction and education.
Br .·. Macé, promoter of that impious league,
had in one month received numerous sub-
scriptions, and *the Masonic World* declared
(February, 1867,) that "*all Masons must give
in their collective adhesion to this beneficent
league,* and that Lodges must study, in the
peaceful retirement of their Temples (sic) the
best means to make it effectual." ·

And there are in France sixteen hundred
thousand Masons! Judge if the danger is
imaginary! Be warned, not only you, Pas-
tors of souls, but you, fathers of family who
are preserving in your heart the least spark
of Faith!

## XXVI.

### How Freemasonry Extends its Action to Young Girls.

Before speaking of feminine Freemasonry,
let us in few words make known a new Ma-

sonic, very dangerous institution : the *professional schools* for young girls.

The professional school's object is to devel-
op primary instruction, and to prepare young
girls belonging to the well-to-do laboring
classes, or to the retail trades, for the different special professions in which they will be
able honorably to make a living. Nothing
better in itself; nothing more useful. Freemasons, understanding how important is the
part of woman in the world, have just found-
ed professional schools in Paris. They have,
it is said, vast projects with regard to this.
Already, two large schools have been opened,
and are carried on under the Lodges' protection. They are conducted by ladies and female teachers enjoying their confidence.

We have nothing to say of the material
side of those Institutions; intelligence and
devotedness can, by themselves, overcome
great difficulties, and bring about serious re-
sults. But, what we must here both show and
lament, is the principle of practical Atheism,
the fundamental principle of Masonry, which
suggests the establishment of those schools;
it is a positive system of religious indiffer-

ence; it is the exclusion of all idea of God,
laid down as the basis of education. In those
schools, it is expressly forbidden to emit a religious idea, however vague and general;
and they are in earnest on that point. Very
recently, a lady teacher, from whose lips the
name of God had inadvertently escaped, was
immediately and unmercifully discharged.
We recognize in that the celebrated *tolerance*
of the free-thinkers.

Those schools are, for girls, a school of
independent Ethics, first of all. They are
a seminary of free females. *The Masonic
World* admires and extols that education.
" As to the morality taught, says it in a report (September, 1866), it is no more Jew-
ish than Protestant; it is *the morality*, that
universal morality which all women and all
men bring with them in this world; " but
which, unfortunately, obscured by original
sin, needs Religion so much, that, without
Religion, there cannot be, there is no morality. Besides, what is morality but the fulfil-
ment of duty? And is it not man's *first duty*
on earth to know his God, to love and serve
Him? This is realized by Religion, but re-

jected by Freemasonry, the pretended morality of which is essentially anti-moral.

There are already more than *three hundred* young girls in the Masonic professional
schools of Paris. Upon which, the same newspaper exclaims: "What are the other cities
of France doing? Why! after such an ex-
ample given by Paris, can we not find in the
principal cities some few *females with an independent mind*, and *free* enough to initiate
this noble devotedness?"

Those schools are the more dangerous because their antichristian character is entirely
negative. What women, what mothers of
family are to come out of them!


## XXVII.

### ABOUT *Adoption* BY FREEMASONRY, OTHER-
WISE, FEMALE FREEMASONRY.

There are female members of Freemasonry.
At first, one will wonder at it, as the main
point is to keep secrets. But Freemasons, it
appears, trust "the women whom they esteem
the most," and to whom they give the pair

of gloves officially presented to themselves by the Venerable.

This feminine Freemasonry seems to date its beginning from the middle of last century. Louis Philippe Egalité, then Duke of Orleans, and Grand-Master of the Order, offered his pair of gloves to Mrs. de Genlis, and gave an extraordinary impulsion to the androgynous Masonry (androgynous means, having the two sexes). Curiosity, love of pleasure, and above all, of the unknown, the spirit of irreligion, and the magical influence of the forbidden fruit, drew to Freemasonry all the ladies who longed to be *free;* and among them were, unhappily, those with the most conspicuous names. A letter from the unfortunate Queen Marie Antoinette to her sister, Queen Marie Christine, dated February 26th, 1781, proves it: " I think that you allow your mind to be too much harassed about Freemasonry . . . Here, every one belongs to it . . . . A few days ago, Princess de Lamballe was made the Grand-Mistress of a Lodge; she related to me all the funny things which she was told."

Alas! poor women! from that very time, the sect was preparing for them the fate intended by it " to Princes, bigots, and noble-men." [1]

Here, as in Freemasonry for men, members saw and heard no more than suited the Chiefs; and Public Authorities, imposed upon, attached no importance to an association which everywhere was viewed as one of beneficence and pleasure only. But, behind the gay meetings, there were infamous mysteries; it was not, as among the men, the worship of vengeance; it was the worship of voluptuousness, the more dangerous because it was veiled by mysterious rites, seasoned with secrets, and flavored by that spirit of irreligion so fashionable in Voltaire's time.

The Lodge of those women was not called a Lodge, but *Temple of Love.* It sounded so lovingly pastoral! The door of the *Temple of Love* was called (no doubt by way of antiphrasis) the door of *Virtue* (through which virtue went away, if not already gone). The Br . ·. Mason who ushered in the postulants, was called Br . ·. *Sentiment* (it is so, word for

---

[1] See Chapter 18th.

word, in the Ritual), and the Mason-Sister who
introduced the aspirants, was called Sister
*Discretion.* The Grand-Master would ask the
one seeking admission : "How old are you ?"
The answer was as innocent as, but more ten-
der than, that of the Brother : "I am seven
years old." To which the sighing dove, gently cooing, added : "1 am old enough to
please and to love." How sweet and charm-
ing !

The male members of that rite were *Knights
of the Rose,* and the female ones *Nymphs of
the Rose.* These *Knights* and *Nymphs* always
went two and two in all their Masonic *works.*
The Temple was all hung with flowers; the
meetings were presided over by a Grand-Master and a Grand-Mistress. No drawn swords,
no papered frames, no caverns, no sombre
masquerades, but, in their place, sentimental
journeys, oaths taken by the female aspirant
in the most gallant manner. She would take
the Grand-Master's seat, whilst he, as a great
simpleton, would be kneeling at her feet. But
the most touching of all was a certain journey
to the *Island of Felicity*, where ended the initiation ; there the bandage was removed from

the *Nymph's* eyes; she found herself before
an altar (O, piety!), before the altar and the
statues (let us say the idols) of Venus and
Cupidon, and she offered incense to the patron and patroness of the Temple.

Assuredly Mrs. de Lamballe and well-
bred Ladies saw in these fiddlefaddles nothing but amusements and gallantries without
consequence; but, for the majority, those
meetings were far from being guiltless; and
the wicked men who secretly conducted that
branch of the Masonic Order, used it to cor-
rupt minds and hearts; to draw away more
and more women from Religion, love of family, respect for authority and for traditions.

The French Revolution drowned in blood
both the *Knights* and *Nymphs of the Rose.*

Under the First Empire, feminine Freemasonry rose from its ashes: nearly all its officers were Masons, and they greatly helped to
revive and to spread all over Europe an institution so marvellously favorable to their irre-
ligious and immoral propensities. In 1830,
new blossoming of female Freemasons. Freemasonry hopes much from woman's co-opera-
tion. "When will it be understood," senti-

mentally exclaims Br ·. Ragon, " that, to re-
store to the Order its irrepressible attractions
and former splendor,— *to public morality, its
purity (!!), and its truth cleared from hypoc-
risy(!!)*,— to domestic education, still over-
run with prejudices, its *humanitary* radiation
—we must admit to Masonic *works* the women,
who, by their virtues (the *virtues* of the free
woman!), honor their sex and their country?
Their presence will make meetings *more interesting;* their speeches (the *speeches* of the
free woman!) will promote emulation; the
*workshops* will be purified, as nature, in the
spring, is purified by the life-giving rays of
a new sun." [1]  Surely, here comes in earnest
the worship of the Sun !

In female Freemasonry, there are, as on the
masculine side, Apprentice, Companion, and
Mistress-Masons. There are also high de-
grees, *Perfect Mistresses, Sublime Scotch, Elect,
Knightesses of the Dove, Knightesses of Joy,
Rosicrucians, or Knightesses of Beneficence,
Princesses of the Crown,* and *Sovereign Masons.*
Unfortunately, Br ·. Pinon's *Annuary* is dis-

[1] *Complete Manual of Masonry by Adoption.* pp. 140, 141.

creetly silent on that columbine branch of
Masonry.

There are rites and a full Ceremonial, as for
the masculine Masonry.   Over the threshold
of the " door of Virtue " is the picture of Mrs.
de Genlis, whom Masonry has  surnamed " *the
Mother of the Church !* "   This chaste Mother
has been, they say, canonized by Philippe-
Egalité.

How curious the homily, stern, but full of
sense, addressed, at the very opening of the
trials, to the postulant, by the Grand-Master,
majestically seated by the side of the Grand-
Mistress !   " He bids her notice *how highly
imprudent* she has been thus to ask, alone
and unsupported, admission *into a Society, the
composition and morals of which are unknown
to her, and where her purity might be endan-
gered.* " [1]

The female Freemasons gird, like the male
members, the famous apron.  The *general* sign,
by which they recognize each other, is very
plain: " hands one over the other, the right
one covering the left and resting on the

[1] Br . · . Ragon : *Complete Manual of Masonry by Adoption*. pp. 25, 26.

apron." They recognize each other as Apprentices " by mutually presenting open the
right hand, with joined fingers, and placing
the palm of the hands one on the other ; " as
Companions, " by mutually taking their right
hand, so that the two thumbs be laid across,
and the middle finger stretched over the
wrist;" as Mistresses, " by presenting to
each other, the index and middle finger of the
right hand, joining them longitudinally, and
on the inside ; then, pressing by turns the
right thumb on the joints of the two fingers,
near the nail." They have other signs, which
truly require a witch's fingers: "To take
(mutually ?) the right ear with the thumb and
the little finger of the right hand, the rest of
the hand being stretched on the cheek (to the
other ear) ; " to take (also mutually ?) the end
of the nose with the thumb and the index of
the right hand, the rest of the hand covering
*both* eyes " (a real feat !) ; " to place the left
hand on the face, the little finger on the mouth,
the ring-finger under the nose, the middle
finger and the index on the eye, and the
thumb on the left ear." The two pass-words
seemingly most in favor with the Mason-Sisters, are *Eva* and *Babel ;* very likely, out of

devotion to the forbidden fruit, and of a very
natural horror for the confusion of *tongues*.
These precious particulars are given by the
grave Br∴. Ragon, the official and sacred
author.

This feminine Masonry is more spread than
one would think; for it numbers many rites
or obediences: the rite of *Cagliostro*, the
rite of *the Scotch Ladies of Mount Thabor*,
the Order of *the Palladium, or Sovereign
Council of Wisdom*, the Order of *Felicity*, the
Order of *the Knights and Knightesses of the
Anchor*, the Order of *Perseverance*, and others besides.

Many more things, and very curious ones,
might be said of the Ladies' Freemasonry.
We shall relate one more, the ceremonial of a
banquet of Mason-Sisters, drawn like the others from the same official source.


## XXVIII.

### A BANQUET OF MASON-SISTERS.

We have before seen that in this Order they
eat and drink much. With ladies, it is as with
men: the sacred banquet, the fraternal ban-

quet, the free banquet is one of the most serious *works* of exterior Freemasonry. According to regulations religiously kept by
those valiant ladies, " they never meet alone ;
they are always helped in their *works* by Masons." In the *work* at table, the male and
female Masons are, therefore, side by side.
" Thus the meeting is far more interesting."
Here is what we read in the Ritual of Br.·.
Ragon :

First the banquet is called *Lodge of Table*.
" There are five obligatory toasts (when coming out of this, the Mason-Sister must often
be merry, and the *free* woman turn to the
*tight* woman). First toast: The Grand-Mistress gives a rap; all mastication stops (sic);
each one conforms to the *table order*, that is,
puts the four fingers of the right hand, joined,
on the table, the thumb being drawn along-
side the edge, and forming the square. She
says : " Dear SS.·. *Inspectress* and *Deposi-
tary*, see that the *lamps* be put on a line and
filled for a toast which the Gr.·. M.·. and I
wish to propose !" The lamps of those free
women are tumblers, drinking tumblers ; from
them they draw light, strength, and liberty.
*Fill the lamp*, means fill the tumbler.

The order being given and fulfilled, S.∴. *Inspectress* says, after having given a rap: " Grand-Mistress, the lamps are on a line and filled."

The Gr.∴. M.∴ raps again, and says: " Up, and to order ! Sword in hand !" and they all take the knife in their left hand. " Beloved BB.∴. and much beloved SS.∴., the toast which it is our privilege and happiness to propose, is : The Kings-Masons ; it is in behalf of healths so dear to our hearts, that we must unite in *blowing our lamps* to their glory ! "

This being said, the Gr.∴. M.∴. *commands the exercise:* " Right hand on the lamps ! hold up the lamps ! Blow the lamps at one draught !" (The Mason-Sister here shows herself to be a woman more and more valiant; she blows her lamp as if it were a match, and drinks like a hole). What dragoons ! If there are *Nymphs of the Rose,* there are also *Nymphs of the Lamp !*

But the *exercise* is not at an end, and the Gr.∴. M.∴. continues : " Lamp forward ! (that is, as explained by the faithful Br.∴. Ragon: five times on the heart, and bring it forward again) "Set down lamps! (which must be done in five times, adds the Ritual). Finally, they say five times Eva." [1]

This is the first toast, the first *exercise* of this warlike banquet. At the fifth one, by dint of *blowing the lamp*, the poor Sister must be staggering, and drawing crooked lines, when going for the twenty-fourth or fifth time " from the heart forward." To go back home, she must need the brotherly arm of her Masonic gossip.

## XXIX.

### DOES FEMININE MASONRY CONFINE ITSELF TO BANQUETS AND AMUSEMENTS?

The sacrilegious and impious Masonic dagger is hidden under the more or less improper amusements of this androgynous Masonry: and secret societies mean to make a very serious use of those silly creatures whom unbelief, pride, vanity, love of pleasure, and especially curiosity, thrust into the exterior

[1] *Complete Manual of Freemasonry by Adoption.* p. 85.

degrees. Like that of men, the public Masonry of women is but a pond in which occult Masonry fattens its fishes to draw them
at the proper time. That time is when the
Mistress-Mason is initiated to the *secret* degree
of *Perfect Mistress.*

First of all, they exact from her the awful
oath which binds her to the Sect for life. "I
swear," she says, "I promise to hold faithfully
in my heart, *the secrets of Freemasons and of
Freemasonry. I bind myself to it under penalty of being cut to pieces by the sword of the
destroying Angel.*"

The Gr∴ M∴ immediately proclaims her
*Perfect Mistress,* and addresses her thus:
" My dear, now that we have initiated you to
the symbolical secret of Masonry, now that
the light of truth has shone forth before your
eyes, the errors, superstitions, and prejudices
(that is, faith and the fear of God) which you
perhaps retained as yet in some corner of
your brains, are removed. An arduous, but
sublime task *is henceforth imposed on you,* (we
come to it; let us listen). *The first of your
duties will be to sour the hearts of the people
against Priests and Kings. In the coffee house,*

*in the theatre, in the evening parties, everywhere,*
*work with that* HOLY *intention.*

"There is one more secret to be revealed
to you, and we shall speak of it in a low tone
of voice." And he declares to her that the
final purpose of the sacred mission of Freemasonry, " is the annihilation of all religious
and monarchical authority."

There is, then, something truly serious in
point, not only of morality, but also of Faith
and the future of the Church, in this ridiculous initiation of women to Freemasonry.
Freemasons know to what advantage women
can be used; they know that woman, once
hurled into the ways of impiety and vengeance, is more savage, and more tenacious
than man, and goes further than he. Is it to
be wondered at, if they are happy to see
women affiliated to their Order, and if they
loudly declare that "to found Lodges for
women, would be going at a giant's rate in
the way of *humanitary* progress?" These
are the words of *the Masonic World*, Oct.,
1866. It is known that their "humanitary
progress" simply is antichristianism.

## XXX.

That the Church has very justly Anathematized the whole Freemasonry, without any Restrictions.

Freemasonry says of itself that it is guiltless, that it is slandered and unjustly condemned by the Church.

We now know enough to appreciate both
the pretended guiltlessness and the pretended
injustice.

Does Masonry believe in the divine authority of the Sovereign Pontiff of the Catholic
Church? No. Does it submit to the Pope in
all things, as commanded by Almighty God?
No; a thousand times no. Does it believe
in the divinity of our Lord Jesus Christ? No.
Does it believe in God, Father, Son, and Holy
Ghost, such as He is, such as He has revealed
Himself to the world, such as He commands
to be adored? No. Therefore, it is, in the
highest degree, guilty of rebellion, impiety,

heresy, blasphemy; therefore it is anticatholic, antichristian, atheist.    Therefore it is condemnable: and when it has been condemned by the Holy See, it has been justly, and very justly, condemned.

In another, less exclusively Christian, point of view, Freemasonry, not only the occult one, rejected by all upright men, but also the one public and exterior, the regulations of which are known, and almost in the hands of the public, is a dangerous institution, wicked, immoral, contrary to the most elementary laws of human justice, and to the welfare of nations.    I bring but one proof: the Masonic oath and the penalty of death as a punishment for its violation.

Freemasonry cannot deny it.    From the very first step of initiation, at the very entering a Lodge through the degree of Apprentice, when falls the bandage, which, until then, has been on the Postulant's eyes, he sees all the drawn swords of the assistants directed against his breast, and he hears all the Brothers shouting:  " May God punish traitors ! " and the Venerable, after having quieted his fears, adds: *"If you were to betray Freema-*

*sonry, no spot on earth could offer you a shelter against its avenging weapons.*" Is this true, or not?—Is it true, or not, that to be a Freemason, to be admitted to that first degree of Apprentice, a man *must* take the abominable oath which we have given at length, textually copied from the Ritual of the Masonic Order?[1]

Those two facts cannot be denied. Now, I ask any upright man, any magistrate: what to think of a private society, which, outside of civil society, in cold blood and officially threatens with death all its members who would be unfaithful to its laws? What to think of a private society, which dares to say : " If you are faithless to me, *no spot on earth could offer you a shelter against my avenging weapons?*" What is that threat, if not a threat of murder and assassination! Now, that is a crime amenable to law in all civilized countries.

What is, I ask it again, this contemptible heap of imprecations which accompany, or, rather, constitute the Masonic oath? Can a

[1] See Chapter 8th.

Christian, a good man, an honest man, in con
science, thus give himself up, soul and body,
under penalty of death, to any society whatever, outside of the holy Church? A society
which forces on all its members, without exception, and receives such an oath,—a private society which, in contempt of all divine
and human laws, attributes to itself such ex-
orbitant rights, and in particular, the right
of life and death on the millions who are
members of it, is a deeply, essentially immoral
society, and the sword of the Church where-
ever it strikes it, strikes it justly.

Thus condemnable, when judged from the
points of view, both of reason and of Faith,
Freemasonry has been justly condemned by
the Holy See, which in this case, as in so
many others, has courageously fulfilled the
salutary mission entrusted to it by Almighty
God. Commissioned to teach all nations, to
proclaim and defend truth, to judge, unmask,
condemn and pursue error and evil, the holy
Church has solemnly anathematized Freemasonry in all its degrees, in all its forms. It
has *excommunicated*, that is, cut off from her
bosom, all Christians, *whoever they are*, who

would dare to affiliate themselves to it, in
spite of her positive prohibition.

Every Freemason, therefore, is, and justly,
excommunicated; the mere Apprentices, as
well as the Grand-Orients, and the Grand-
Masters, the high and the low, the female and
the male Freemasons, the members of Lodges,
as well as the adepts of the back Lodges.

## XXXI.

### EXPRESS SENTENCES PASSED ON FREEMASONRY
### BY THE SOVEREIGN PONTIFFS.

Our Lord Jesus Christ has said in the Gospel: *If any one does not hear the Church, let him
be to you as a heathen.* Now, the Church, by
the grand voice of the Popes, has solemnly
and expressly condemned Freemasonry.

As far back as the first half of last century, when Masonry was more openly organized in Europe, Pope Clement the XIIth, condemned it in a Bull, dated April 23d, 1738.
"Reflecting," says the Pope, "on the great
evils with which those clandestine societies
threaten, either the peace of States, or the

salvation of souls, after having consulted our
Venerable Brethren the Cardinals, of our own
accord, and in the fulness of Apostolical power, we have enacted and decreed that the
aforesaid societies, assemblies, or meetings of
*Freemasons*, whichever name they take, must
be condemned and proscribed, as we do condemn and proscribe them by the present constitution, the effect of which is to last forever." " To this end," he adds, " by virtue of
holy obedience, we forbid all and every
Christian faithful, of whatever profession,
dignity or condition, clergymen or laymen,
secular or regular, to establish, propagate or
favor the society called *Freemasons*, to admit
it in their houses, to be affiliated to it, and to
assist at its meetings, *under penalty of excommunication to be incurred, ipso facto, without
any new declaration*, and especially reserved
to us and to our successors, so that no one
can absolve from it without our permission,
except at the point of death."

During the reign of Benedict the XIVth,
some persons endeavored to make it believed
that the Constitution of Clement the XIIth,
was no more binding, and that those who then

were affiliated to the society of Freemasons, did not incur excommunication. After seriously examining the question, the illustrious Pontiff hastened to undeceive them, and by his Bull of May 28th, 1751, he confirmed his predecessor's Constitution in all its injunctions. "That no one may accuse us," says he, " to have failed in what prudence requires of us, we have resolved to re-issue our predecessor's Constitution, by inserting it word for word in our present letters ; thus acting with clear knowledge, and by virtue of the fulness of Apostolical power, we confirm it, we re-issue it, and we order and decree that it be, from this day, put to execution, as if it were now published for the first time."

The Society of Carbonari so called, which, at the beginning of this century, spread all over Europe, and especially over Italy, was, as we have seen, but a ramification of Freemasonry. In his Bull of Sept. 13th, 1821, Pope Pius the VIIth, describes its main features ; he shows its intimate connection with the Masonic Order ; he indicates all the evils to be feared from it for Religion and Christian society ; and those evils have been but too much realized ever since until now. By that Constitution, the Venerable Pius the VIIth, decrees the same penalty of excommunication, especially reserved to the Apostolic See, against all those who would join it or favor it in any way whatever.

In 1825, Pope Leo the XIIth, viewing all secret societies in their whole, was terrified at the thought of all the evils which Religion and the State had to fear from them; he saw with an inexpressible grief that in them religious indifference was preached, that they received men of all religions and of all beliefs; that they assumed the right of life and death over those who broke the secrets of the Lodges, or refused to fulfil the criminal orders given to them; he was appalled at the deep contempt shown by them for all authority. Consequently, in his Bull of March 13th, 1825, he republished, in a most express manner, the Constitutions issued against secret societies, and particularly against Freemasons, by his predecessors, Clement the XIIth, Benedict the XIVth, and Pius the VIIth, and forbade, as they did, all the faithful to affiliate themselves to them, and to join them in any

9

way whatever, under penalty of excommunication *ipso facto*, and especially reserved to
the Holy See, so that the Pope alone could
absolve from it, except in case of death.

Lastly, in his Allocution of Sept. 1865, our
Holy Father, Pope Pius the IXth, deplores,
as his predecessors, all the evils inflicted on
the Catholic Religion, and on Christian civilization by the secret societies in general, and
in particular by that of the Freemasons. He
republishes all the dispositions contained in
the Apostolical Constitutions of Popes Clement the XIIth, Benedict the XIVth, Pius the
VIIth, and Leo the XIIth, and especially
the penalty of excommunication laid on all
those who are affiliated to them, or who favor
them in any way. He exhorts the faithful
who might have had the misfortune to be received in them, to leave them forthwith, in order to save their souls, and, at the same time,
he strongly exhorts those who, so far, were
fortunate enough to stay away from them,
never to allow themselves to be drawn into
that dangerous abyss.

Therefore, doubt is now impossible; all
those who are affiliated to the society of Free-

masons, by the very fact of their affiliation, incur the penalties laid on them, by Clement the XIIth, in 1738; by Benedict the XIVth, in 1751; by Pius the VIIth., in 1821; by Leo the XIIth, in 1825; and by Pope Pius the IXth, in Sept., 1867. They are expressly excommunicated; they have no more any share in the prayers of the Church; they must not any more assist at the Holy Sacrifice of the Mass, nor at the other public services; nor can they receive any sacrament. If they die in that state, they forfeit all rights to ecclesiastical burial, because the Church does not count them any more among her Children.

Either Catholic or Freemason, there is no choice. "One cannot be Freemason and Catholic at the same time."[1]

## XXXII.

### WHAT WE MUST DO, IN THE FACE OF THE GREAT ANTI CHRISTIAN CONSPIRACY.

The Church is so powerfully constituted, that she has but to be herself to thwart *all* the plots of *all* her enemies. Let us, one and

[1] *The Masonic World*, May, 1866. p. 6.

all, be but Christians, earnest Catholics, and we stand ready.

Union begets strength. Our enemies understand it; their strength is in their union, and their union is in their obedience. Let us be united more than they are ; and, for that purpose, let us obey better than they do. The whole Catholic Church can be summed up in two words: Obedience and Love. Let us obey with love; let us love through obedience.

First of all and above all, let us obey *in all things* the head of the Holy Church, our Holy Father, the Pope, Vicar of Jesus Christ, Pastor and Infallible Teacher of all Christians.

Surely to obey the Pope, let us obey our Bishop, our Parish Priest, our Confessor. When we obey them, we obey not men, but God himself, who, through them, teaches us, guides us, forgives us, and makes us walk in the right path. As much Masonic obedience is blind, silly, absurd, wicked and sacrilegious, so much Catholic obedience is grounded on reasoning, rational, legitimate, holy, and meritorious. What is nobler than to obey God?

To obedience let us add love. The soul of

union is love. Let us love one another, chris-
tianly, efficaciously; if we are rich, let us love
and assist the poor; they are our brothers,
and in their person we love and assist Jesus
Christ. Let us love our Priests, and surround them with all marks of respect; let us
love our Bishop, the Father and the Pastor
of our souls; and more yet, let us love the
Pope. Here is *true fraternity*, of which Masonic fraternity is but the impious disguise,
as their liberty and their equality are but the
disguise of true Christian liberty, and of true
equality. Men are truly equal only before
God; they are truly free only when becoming the children of God.

Freemasonry attacks us through "the
Press;" let us be on our guard; let us never
read bad newspapers; let us acquire a thor-
ough knowledge of the truths of Faith; if
able, let us scatter around us good Catholic
books. A good book is a Missionary; and
very often, people are converted by reading
it.

Freemasonry aims at wresting from us the
souls of our children; let us react with the utmost energy, and from evil let us draw good.
Let us kindle anew our zeal for the salvation

and sanctification of our children, for their instruction, and to prepare them to be valiant soldiers of the Church. Fathers and mothers, do not forget that God has entrusted you with the care of their souls, and that education, if not thoroughly Christian, is now, more than ever, an immense danger for them.

Finally, let us revive around us the family spirit, the love of family, in place of which the Masonic sects seek to put we know not what pretended patriotic chimera, good only to unduly excite imagination, and turn one's head. Let us be fully convinced of this: the remedy against all the Masonic venom, consists exclusively in being true Christians, in substituting humility, obedience, and faith to pride, in truly loving our Lord Jesus Christ with all our heart, with all our soul, with all our strength.

If we do not act so, we have all to fear; yes, all to fear in this world and in the next. If, on the contrary, we remain faithful to God and to His Church, we have nothing to fear; the future is ours.

The struggle which is coming is either the supreme struggle of the Church, or it is not.

If the former, the Church, as foretold, will succumb for a time, as Christ on Calvary; and we shall succumb with her; but, as on Calvary, Satan shall be defeated, and all his party shall be hurled into the place of everlasting torments, the Freemasons no less than any other; we, on the contrary, rising in glory forever, shall go to Heaven, there eternally to reign with our Lord Jesus Christ. If the latter, we must look at the struggle with a yet more cheerful confidence; for the enemy who stands across our path, may win some partial triumphs; but soon the storm shall blow over, as so many before; and even in this world, we shall ourselves enjoy with the Holy Church, victory and peace.

In either case, our duties are the same : union, obedience, lively faith, fraternal charity, zeal for the salvation of souls, and the holy cause of the Church.

All of us, let us fight the good fight, under the glorious banner of the Immaculate Virgin, and of St. Peter!

THE END.

*Freemasonry seeks, above all, silence and darkness. Its first care, when attacked, is to be silent, and play dead. In Belgium, it has been an invariable watch-word for some years past. It is the same, it would seem, in France and everywhere. Let us, therefore, raise our voice, and without tiring, loudly cry: danger, danger!*

*Would it not be a good work to make this small treatise known all around, and to spread it as much as possible?*